COLLECTED
ESSAYS OF
Ervin
Seale

Mentors of New Thought Series

COLLECTED
ESSAYS OF
Ervin
Seale

 DeVorss Publications

ISBN: 0-87516-682-2

Library of Congress Catalog Card No.: 95-69031

Printed in the United States of America

DeVorss & Company, *Publishers*
Box 550
Marina del Rey, CA 90294-0550

Contents

A Note

FOR OVER A DECADE through the 1960s and 1970s, Milton Cross introduced a "religious triumvirate" each Sunday night on WOR Radio in New York City. This threesome was Bishop Fulton Sheen, Reverend Norman Vincent Peale and Doctor Ervin Seale, each delivering 30-minute talks on subjects of his own choosing. Dr. Seale stated that the theme of his talks was "Healthy-mindedness and how to find peace in this constantly changing world."

With the exception of "Your Mind Is a Magnet," "Employ God," and the essays of single-page length, this collection gathers some of the very best of Doctor Seale's radio talks, whose 30-minute format challenged him to organize his philosophy into succinct statements that, decades later, continue to afford inspiration, encouragement, and renewed reason for living in a still "constantly changing world."

COLLECTED
ESSAYS OF
Ervin
Seale

Your Mind
Is a Magnet

For though we walk in the flesh we do not war after the flesh:

For the weapons of our warfare are not carnal, but mighty through God to the pulling down of strongholds;

Casting down imaginations, and every high thing that exalteth itself against the knowledge of God, and bringing into captivity every thought to the obedience of Christ.

—2 Cor. 10:3–5

THERE IS A WAY of happiness and there is a way of sorrow. One is the knowledge of this world. The other is the wisdom called Christ in the Bible. Let no one who reads Paul's letter to the Corinthians suppose that Paul is preaching the theories of a man. Christ is not a particular man. Christ is an understanding, a wisdom which was possessed by the man Jesus. There are many kinds of knowledge, and men are known by the knowledge

3

they possess. There is Smith, the portrait painter, Jones, the engraver, Williams, the navigator. Each of these is initiated into a knowledge which other men do not have. If any man wished to be a portrait painter of the Smith school, he would have to go to Smith and let Smith teach him. Until that time he is in ignorance of a knowledge which Smith alone possesses.

Well, Christ is the highest wisdom. It is the way of health and happiness. Paul has had the revelation of this Christ and he is preaching it to the Corinthians. This is not Paul the religious zealot preaching a new doctrine or a new creed or the teachings of a certain historical man to some people whom he hopes to make converts to this new sect. For Christ is not a sect and Christ is not a creed. Christ is a knowledge of the inner processes of man by means of which his life here is made easier and happier. It is the knowledge that your consciousness is the maker and governor of all your activities and accomplishments. Paul is preaching Christ to the Greeks but he is not preaching a *man*. A *man* cannot save you. Only the wisdom which Jesus knew can save you. Jesus was the man, and Christ was his wisdom, Christ is what Jesus knew—his understanding.

In the Scriptures the Greeks are the intellectuals of the world. The Greek nation at that time represented the highest in learning and instruction from an external standpoint. These are the wise men of the world and they become symbolical in the scriptural story of the ''wise men,'' so-called, of all ages. The ''wise men'' of this world, those who are schooled in the knowledge of matter and its ''laws,'' are those who believe that there are certain forces in nature which are inimical to man's good or which can oppose his happiness—the common belief that pollen causes hay fever, that wet feet will bring a cold, that other men hurt you or prevent your happiness, that a certain diet will make you healthy while you dwell in an unhealthy state of mind. These are the opinions and beliefs of the world, and the science of the world is built upon them. A great mass of evidence is piled up to prove these theories.

But there is a wisdom above and beyond all this which shows that man's consciousness is the sovereign and ruler of his own world, that there are no outside powers, that there is no disease outside of his own mind, that no experience can befall him without his consent. This is Christ, the king of sciences and the queen of arts. Man sometimes gives his consent because he is ignorant of Christ. The wisest men of this world may be, and often are, ignorant of Christ. So the eternal story tells of a man who has seen it, coming to preach to those who have not. "We preach Christ crucified, unto the Jews a stumbling-block and unto the Greeks foolishness" (1 Cor. 1:23).

To the Greeks (those who are filled with the knowledge of this world) the teaching of Christ is foolishness. The modern Greek is found everywhere. He is the man or woman who knows many things which aren't true. He has his beliefs, and anything which contradicts them is foolishness. He knows that he gets hay fever every July and it is foolishness to his very logical mind to say that his hay fever is in his consciousness and nowhere else. A modern Paul will come preaching to him and say, Get understanding and your sickness will pass. This is nonsense to him for he is very wise. The mind that is full cannot be taught. A man will often hold on to his beliefs, even though they bring him to his grave in misery, rather than admit that the cause is in himself. So one must become as receptive and as meek as a little child before the wisdom of Christ can enter.

This wisdom is a stumbling-block to the Jews. In the New Testament the Jews are those who look for a prophet to come. It does not mean just a race or a religious group. The modern Jew looks for a time to come when he will be happy. He wails in anguish now and commiserates with his friends about the hardness of the world; but, he says, sometime we shall all be happy.

He hopes for some saviour to come and get him out of his difficulty. Not knowing that he himself is the cause of his difficulty, he is also ignorant of the fact that he, himself, is his own saviour. He cannot see that the saviour has already come and is here. I Am is his name. He is not a man but the living spirit of the living God which is in man, and which is all that is real of man. To this "Jew" of all ages and all climes the teaching of Christ is a stumbling-block. He cannot comprehend it. Being unconscious of any power in his own possession, he ascribes power to things outside himself. Place before him the rock of Truth and he stumbles. He cannot work this wisdom into the structure of his life.

If you are truly "in Christ" you are in a new understanding of yourself and all the world about you. You are not just worshiping a man and saying, "We are saved by Christ." How are you saved? Are you saved from your illness because you adopt a creed and say, I believe in Jesus Christ, the only Lord and saviour? Or, if you come into New Thought and say, I accept the Christ of myself—are you saved by saying that? You must demonstrate your prophet or you have no prophet.* You may say, I believe in Muhammad, or I am a follower of the Buddha, or of Confucius. Well, let me see the strong qualities of Muhammad in you and I'll agree that you believe in him. Let me see the peace of the Buddha in you or the wisdom of Confucius and I can tell whether you are a true follower of these. The prophet we believe in must always be demonstrated, and it is a way of living; it is a wisdom above this world. It is a scientific understanding of the spirit in you as cause and your environment as result. It is the knowledge that when you take hold of an idea and induce the mood of it, you have started the movement of the spirit of God relative to that idea and it will create itself according to a law which the mind of man cannot fathom. When the clouds of

* See "Demonstrate Your Prophet," p. 88.

your mortal knowledge break and roll aside, then, out of these clouds will come the understanding which is Christ, to save you. Sometimes, to you as to all men, the light will break. You will be thrown to your knees like Paul, and out of the invisible a voice will speak to you and direct you. You will walk blind for a while, for the light will be too great for sight. But you will emerge from the experience changed in name and nature. You will date your life from this experience. Heretofore you have not lived. Now life will begin anew in another world. You will begin to preach the gospel of Christ in your living.

The gospel means literally the "good spell." All men's minds are under spells. What is your spell now? Tell me how you feel and I'll tell you what spell you operate under. Is your dominant mood as you walk through life the mood of joy and confident expectancy? Do you like your work? Do you love your family? In general, are you happy? If so, you are under a good spell. On the other hand, if things and people disturb you and take your peace, if you get discouraged easily and melancholy often comes to dwell with you, then you are living under an evil spell. Every idea and thought casts its spell upon the mind and induces some emotion. Men are moved by these emotions and not by intelligence or science. The world thinks it lives by its wits, but it really lives by the spells that are cast upon men's minds by ignorance. Any idea which stirs a man's emotions will make him move toward the execution of the idea. Since most of the ideas that stir men are negative and destructive, the race moves through sorrow and distress.

Now, the science of Christ is the understanding that you have control over your emotions through your power to choose the ideas with which you live. You are exhorted to have in you that mind which was also in Jesus Christ (Philippians 2:5). The mind of Christ is a mind that knows that the individual consciousness controls all phenomena in the individual world. It is a disciplined mind which will not give ear to anything but good.

When harm is predicted, it reverses the picture. It is confident of its own power which is the power of God. The ignorant man, when told that he is about to fall sick, will induce fear and create the things he fears. The enlightened man, knowing the greatness of God, will defy the prophecies of ignorance and will live. The spell that you cast or allow to be cast on your mind is like a magnet. It pulls to you things like itself. As magnetized steel draws other steel and not copper or nickel, so the mood of confidence will draw conditions that make you confident and happy. For example, a person has certain ambitions and desires. Let him acquaint himself with the Truth of God until he is able to trust this power to realize all his desires, until he is able to control all unruly emotions and sustain the moods of peace, confidence and inner happiness. If you chart the life of such a person over a period of time, you will find that there will be no expression, experience or event in his outer experience which will bring him other than satisfaction. A man's experiences are the exact and mathematical reflection of the moods or spells in which he lives. The spirit is the only creator. The way the spirit creates in you and relative to you is the way you feel.

Paul counsels, "Bring in captivity every thought to the obedience of Christ." The Christ understanding is the great magnet which imparts its nature to every idea that touches it. What is your idea of your health? When you think of your health, what is the nature of your thought? Do you still hold some of the beliefs of the world in regard to your body—that other powers can make it ill without your consent? Then take this concept of your body to the wisdom which is Christ. Examine it in this light. You will then discover all the flaws in this erroneous opinion you hold. Remember that your consciousness is the only power relative to your world. What are you conscious of? If fear or despair, then change it. Contemplate yourself as you wish to be, healthy and happy. Accept this in your mind and accept nothing less. Lose your fear in any other so-called power. Be strong and defiant of any false beliefs. Repose all of your confidence in the power of God moving as your feeling. Now you have brought the idea of your body into the captivity of the Christ understanding. What is your idea of your work? Here is a new business setting up in competition. What do you think of it? Are you afraid it will take business from you? Then remember that there is no competition anywhere except in your own mind. The only competition there is, is the competition between your idea of success and your idea of failure. Review the principles of the Christ science and see that your success is dependent upon nothing outside but only upon your firmness in trusting the subjective power that does all things. Thus do you bring the idea of your success into captivity to the Christ wisdom. This idea is charged with Truth and happiness. It is magnetized with goodness and it will move through all your enterprise from office to factory and bring experiences and results which are like itself.

All of this is simply a scientific way of praying or, as we say in New Thought, "treating." To be scientific you must be convinced that the only creative power is your own consciousness. This leaves no room for the beliefs and opinions of men. It rules out all beliefs in the weather, in germs, in other men's thoughts or actions and removes your allegiance to these as powers which have any rule over your life. Therefore, as the Scripture says, Cast down all imaginations and everything that exalteth itself against the knowledge of God. Allow no idea to be the subject of your meditation which does not induce the spell of peace and happiness. Every morning as you rise to take up the affairs of the day, qualify every act and thought with your best understanding of the law of Christ. Magnetize every idea, proposition and project with the wisdom that is called Christ and send them into your world like magnets to draw to you the experiences that reflect the nature of the idea you thought and felt. They carry their own power with them. Let them work. Do not struggle. Trust God. Covet above all things that quiet peace in the heart that knows no fear. Strive for composure and inward joy. This is your great task. God will do the rest. Christ's way is without effort. Heaven is the state of peace you enter in your prayers. Go to this heaven often and the heaven you idealize will come to you.

The Devil and Your Mind

WHY DID THIS happen to *me*? is a question that is most frequently asked of me in the consultation room. Especially when sickness comes. What did I do to deserve this? Why does God disapprove of me? What is my sin? When evils mount up and reverses are multiplied the vexed sufferer asks, "Who or what has it in for me?"

Religion has answered these questions by saying that God is good and God is love; then evil must be another power, a power of evil called the Devil. Because we humans think first of all in images before we develop the ability of abstract thought, man has made images of this God and this Devil. God is a benign, gentle but stern old man with a long white beard, sitting somewhere in the heavens, and the Devil is a half-human individual with cloven hoofs for feet, bat-like ears on his head, a long tail which stings, and he carries a weapon which can pierce. Such beings have never been seen by human beings. They are the projections of human thinking. These are the mental images with which the human mind has attempted to conceive of the forces of good and evil. This process of making images of the forces and functions we find in ourselves and in our environment —and then projecting these images outward beyond ourselves as separate identities and entities—is the primitive and childish way of thinking.

All thinking begins this way. We are sensate beings and our first experience is sensation of the world around us. After sensation comes reaction of pain or pleasure, satisfaction or dissatisfaction. We either like it or we do not like it and if we do not like it, we have to account for it. So after our reaction comes our interpretation or explanation of the phenomenon. At this level of thinking the explanation usually takes the form of "some other" than ourselves, which is the source or cause of our pleasure or our pain. Thus we attribute pleasure to the gods and pain to the devils and since we have not yet learned to think abstractly, we image these forces and make pictures of them in our minds, giving them a local identity and character and endowing them with a power which afterwards we shall see is none other than our own.

For example, things happen to us in life; we stub a toe or a draft makes us sneeze or a man plays with his children and breaks a leg; we eat something and the stomach is upset, we struggle and strive valiantly and we fail, we try to live justly and amiably but other people in the family or in the nation or in the world provoke us and make trouble. To each and all of these we react. Because we are alive and sensate or sensible we have to react. Our first reaction is pain, disappointment and disapproval, perhaps fear and anger and hate. Then, as the pressure mounts up, comes inquiry and finally explanation and conclusion. Unfortunately, the explanation often comes from another or from others who have no more understanding of the situation than ourselves, yet because we believe them and take them for an "authority" we accept their illusions and delusions as an explanation of our misery or our pain. The skeptic, the cynic and the iconoclast have all found out something that is not so, that is not true, and have resolutely refused to go on to find out what is true. Ignorance must give way to information and wisdom. We stumble and hurt ourselves when we walk in the darkness. We must have the light.

I offer here the Bible's view of one power operating and manifesting in its twofold capacity. The Bible teaches that there is just one creative power, not two, not ten, not twenty, not a hundred, but just one. The Bible teaches that this power both wounds and heals, kills and makes alive. When it operates in a constructive manner it is called God and when it operates in a destructive manner it is called the Devil. Every other force we know on this earth works exactly in this way. Electricity, for example can warm us or kill us. A little acid can maim the flesh or etch a beautiful picture on glass or metal. A flowing river can rush headlong to the sea and flood its banks and destroy life and property and erode the soil, but when dammed and contained and channeled through a turbine it can light cities and turn the wheels of industry.

All objects and forces in this world are good and bad, not in themselves but according to the use to which they are put, and the use to which all are put is determined by the thought of the mind that uses them or relates itself to them. Thus the mind is the executive and determining force and good or bad is not to be postulated of things and natural forces, but rather of the thought or the mind that uses these forces. This is a concept which every good working metaphysician must learn and learn thoroughly, else his position will be weak to the extent that he does not understand this. Unseeing minds are always arguing the point with those of us who teach it, trying to insist in their small way that there are creative forces and entities outside of man himself. They seem to want to justify their own hurts and failures by explaining them in terms of another cause than themselves. But life will not allow you to get away with this.

How often do we attribute our sickness to the air we breathe, the food we eat, or the environment we live in, or the thoughts and acts of other people, or the germs or viruses that float in the air! We will believe in an invisible virus, which no one has ever seen, before we will believe in our own invisible mind and spirit power, which likewise no one has ever seen. And when such beliefs become sovereign and authoritarian in the mind, they rule and govern the experience of the individual; and as the Scripture says, "According to your faith, be it done unto you." When these erroneous beliefs and opinions and illusions are enthroned in the mind, Lucifer, or the Devil, is said to rule, and Lucifer is the false light. When illumination and wisdom come to the mind and the darkness vanishes, then Lucifer is said to fall. "How art thou fallen from heaven, O Lucifer, son of the morning! How art thou cut down to the ground, which didst weaken the nations! For thou hast said in thine heart, I will ascend into heaven, I will exalt my throne above the stars of God: I will sit also upon the mount of the congregation, in the sides of the north." Error and untruth and false opinion and misinformation always act this way in the human mind. Stiff-necked and proud, argumentative, defiant, they throw their weight around and claim to be supreme.

So exults Lucifer in those who think they have caught me in a trap and have disproved my theory that there is only one power. Actually I have no theory of my own. I read this truth in the Bible. I observe life from this point of view and see this truth corroborated at every turn. And every time you analyze the phenomenon or the experience far enough you will see that there is just one executive, primary, creative cause behind all things —and then Lucifer will tumble from the throne in your mind. "Thou shalt be brought down to hell, to the sides of the pit. They that see thee shall narrowly look upon thee and consider thee, saying, Is this the man that made the earth to tremble, that did shake kingdoms; that made the world as a wilderness,

and destroyed the cities thereof; that opened not the house of his prisoners? . . . thou hast destroyed thy land, and slain thy people.''
To sum up, in all cases of limitation, you will find the mind in limitation. Not necessarily a mind that *believes* in limitation but nevertheless a mind which is existing in limitation, perhaps unconsciously.
In all of this the adversary is ignorance or carelessness, neglect, or erroneous knowledge in ourselves. This false occupant of the throne inside is called the Devil or ''the adversary.'' It is the individual's own sense of limitation or boundary. It is not an entity separate and apart. It is not an intelligence apart from the mind of man. It has no existence outside of the consciousness of man. When one does not believe in his own indwelling Christ or power to do and to be and to have, the degree to which he does not believe is the Devil who is the source of all his hurt and evil. Christ is the Truth or the working knowledge of the God power within a man, and ''Christ has made us free from the law of sin and death.''
Go over these concepts again and again and make them clear and strong in you. Establish them as strong convictions which will rule and govern in your thought. Then your treatments and your prayers will be with power and you will find yourself and your life less and less under the scourge, and more and more triumphant, yourself and all your concerns being led in the paths of peace and in the ways of pleasantness.

How to Live
Here and Now

SOME TIME AGO I wrote a little piece entitled, "The Twain Are One," meaning that Spirit and matter are one and God and man are one and Thought and thing are one. The piece said, "At times men have denied the existence of Spirit and robbed mankind of their wings. Other men have denied the existence of matter and taken away the very legs we stand on. Let there be no needless conflict between soul and body. They must exist in harmony. Body is not a hindrance or a prison but a wonderful vehicle for learning and expression. Welcome and enjoy the material life in order to accomplish the higher development of the spiritual nature."

Now I have a letter in which the writer says that the piece quoted is confusing. The letter asks, "Doesn't true spirituality consist in getting away from the world and worldliness? And didn't Gandhi teach us to renounce the world?" And, of course, I must answer that true spirituality does not consist in getting away from the world. Quite the reverse. Our task is to live in the world but be not of it. You cannot take God, the All Good,

16

and put Him on a shelf away from the world of sight and sound and smell and taste and call God good and the world ugly. Yet there has always been a strong tendency in Christianity to do just this and it develops what the psychologists call ambivalence or a conflict in the mind and soul of man. Neither did Gandhi teach this. Gandhi said, "Renounce the world and take it back on different terms." That is the secret of true spirituality and true creative evolution and true power and peace in your personal life. To renounce the world you have to let go of some of your opinions and attitudes about it and reinterpret its processes and then take it back and live in it without pain and without fear.

When our experiences in the physical world become onerous and difficult, then it is time to make our contact with the Causative Power of all material phenomena. In other words, we have to give some attention to the inside world, the world of thought and feeling, the spiritual world. The growing person discovers a precise relationship between his thoughts and his experiences; therefore he learns to have quiet times and prayer times wherein he makes his thoughts and feelings right and aligns them with the Divine Order. Then he relaxes and allows the Divine Order and the Divine Law to run its calming and strengthening influence through all of his acts and through all of the events of his life. Our job here is to make a harmony between the spiritual and the material, to see that since one is the faithful expression of the other, it is our privilege to make it as beautiful and happy an expression as possible by learning to think more truly and more constructively.

Answer the material world's demands in the best way that you can at the place where you are; but when the physical world lays great burdens upon you, like pain and suffering or frustration and obstruction, then render unto God the things that are God's. That is, pray and get your mind and heart in order. Think about freedom and advancement and Divine Order, and since the physical world is an expression of the spiritual world, you will soon find these qualities and characteristics in the physical world.

You and I must learn that we are spirit and body, and that they are one; that the Spirit is the Divinity within us and it shapes our ends; that judgment is given unto man and by his judgments he directs the spirit into new forms and bodies. Let us learn not to look down our noses at material things, to divorce the Spirit from the dust and dirt and the messy house of flesh and blood. And let us learn not to dismiss the Spirit as an airy nothing of no consequence in this practical, material world. The two in union are responsible for the dynamics of the whole world. Every physical act, no matter how vulgar or vile by your description or mine, is sacramental in the sense that it is the Spirit animating material form. The material world in itself is not demeaning nor can it contaminate us in any way. But there is a strong tendency in many people to think that certain aspects of the material world are ugly and that certain kinds of labor are degrading and that they themselves are demeaned when they do these tasks.

Recently, for example, a housekeeper in a fashionable midtown hotel told me of her troubles in hiring maids. One applicant was assigned to be the bathmaid whose duty it is to clean the bathroom fixtures. When shown her tasks, she objected, saying, "I don't clean no toilet bowls for nobody." So another old hand, already overburdened because she is a willing, enthusiastic worker, was called in to do the immediate bathroom jobs and she did them with glory in her heart. Her work is sacramental. Another applicant for the maid's job objected to getting down on the floor and said, "I don't get down on my knees to scrub floors."

Well, somebody will get down on his or her knees, because floors must be scrubbed. This is one of the world's demands upon humanity, and humanity must answer it or have no houses and floors and allow civilization to go backward. Sometimes the most spiritual souls are found doing menial jobs because they do them with a glory in their heart and rejoice in making the atoms and molecules of a material world obey their righteous will and purpose.

There is a story about Lincoln that tells us that when a visiting statesman was ushered into his presence he found the President blacking his own shoes. "So, Mr. President," said the visitor, "you black your own boots?" "Yes," said Lincoln; "whose boots do you black?"

At one time or another some sect has put the finger of prohibition on nearly every item of food and drink. Many have put it upon sex, some on cards and dancing, and musical instruments in the church, and various kinds of dress. The catalogue of these prohibitions and proscriptions is endless, and the conflicts and miseries arising from them are too awful to imagine. Our health suffers greatly when we despise matter. Look at these things called allergies. There are people who fall ill at the sight of cucumbers, asparagus, mushrooms, feathers, whiskey, cigarettes, eggs, cabbages and cats. But a physician friend assures me that he never knew of anyone who was allergic to money! All people seem to have made their at-one-ment with that. So great is their at-one-ment or union with money that it casts out their fear. Certainly money travels about a lot and gets into the most curious and dirty places. Yet few of us will refuse a piece of money on that account. If we were to walk down the street scattering five- and ten- and twenty-dollar bills freely but announcing plainly that each was contaminated with tubercular bacilli, not any would be left lying around. If we can do it with money, we can do it with all things. That man is proof against the invasion of disease without who has no disease within. He will have no disease within if often he dedicates his thoughts, his desires, his purpose to Truth and to right order and invokes upon himself the consciousness that the Spirit is God and the

Spirit is in him, that its law is harmony or love, and so long as he observes this law, he is free to use the Spirit powerfully and with great enterprise and go forward in victory and accomplishment. But he must keep the balance and not resent or despise the world. This physical world is the workshop of the Spirit. *Your* physical world is the workshop of *your* spirit, and your spirit can do things with the matter of your life. Tomorrow, for example, you will be out there in the world of matter, away from the peace and the comfort of the room in which you are now reading. You will be knee-deep, hip-deep or ear-deep in the matter of this world, handling the material stuff of life—money, cloth, bricks, food and the merchandise thereof. There will be voices shouting and arguing, telephones jangling, machines humming. There will be confusion and pressure. Take a moment now and then to remember that your spirit is capable of handling all of this. Your spirit is capable of guiding it, of molding it, directing it, shaping it and extruding it into profitable and pleasurable forms and expressions. Hear the Spirit within you saying, ''I came that ye might have life and have it more abundantly,'' and then allow no private opinion of your own to deny this heavenly and lordly announcement.

This physical world is the playground of the Spirit wherein it is disporting itself for pleasure. Help it to have fun. That is its purpose here. Spirit does not grow. It is complete now. But its forms and expressions grow and change and grow again. Don't judge by the forms. Judge by the Spirit and do not despise the forms while they are growing. The Spirit without the form is nothing, and the form without Spirit is nothing, but the two together—they are Life. ''Today well lived makes every yesterday a dream of happiness and every tomorrow a vision of hope.''

Emotions
We Live By

AN AUTOMOBILE RUNS on gasoline, an electric motor is fed by current, a body is fueled on food and the human psyche is nourished by emotions. A person requires a certain amount of emotional life in order to feel alive at all. The principal life-giving emotions are confidence and courage, love and peace and joy. Each person requires his quota of these life-giving emotions, and when they are plentiful he thrives, he feels fulfilled and he does his work well and he sleeps well. But where these are absent in a personality, to the extent that they are absent, that person does not thrive and is generally ineffective. For many, many people, these healthy emotions are not readily available. If they ever had them, they have lost them, and their psychic currents have been short-circuited. In the place of these positive emotions the negative ones rule instead, and it ought to be pointed out right here that a negative emotion is simply the absence of a positive opposite emotion. A negative emotion is not a thing to fight; it is something to be supplanted. Fear and anxiety and hopelessness are not real things in themselves; they are denials of a positive opposite, and it is that positive opposite that the nervous and fearful person ought to search for with all his heart, zeal and vigor. Negative emotions mean that the gas tank is empty or nearly so. It must be filled; and to be filled, it must be taken to the source. And the source is the spiritual truth that man is a spiritual being and that he is free, that persons, places, things and circumstances do not rule and govern—it is only his reaction to these things that determines how a person lives and what he does and how he feels. "God in the midst of thee is mighty." That means that the essential truth of one's being is capable of handling all of the problems and circumstances of human existence, and to keep on knowing this builds emotional sovereignty and fills the consciousness with those basic positive emotions I mentioned before.

Consider one way in which this is taught symbolically but ingeniously in the Old Testament. The account says that when the tribes returned from captivity to Jerusalem, they were enrolled according to their genealogy; that is, they had to be able to trace their ancestry back to Abraham. If they could not tell their genealogy or ancestry, they were excluded. This is a metaphor or a figure of a great truth, and that great truth is this: Our genealogy is from God. God is our Father. If you are proud of your human ancestors, that is good because it gives you strength and pride and courage and confidence. But it is not enough, for, as someone long ago pointed out, the only good belonging to you may be underground. But if you know your true Father, your spiritual source, then you are noble, free, enfranchised forever. The old writing says that a bastard shall not enter into the congregation because he does not know his father. This is not to be taken literally, but rather psychologically. A man who does not know his physical father is not, on that account, inferior to one who does. But one who does not know his spiritual source and therefore the heritage with which he is endowed cannot enter the company of free and happy men because he is bound in fears and anxieties and hatreds and angers and resentments. This is the only real captivity into which anyone can go. It is the emergence from this kind of captivity that all are seeking, whether they know it or not. You may have been a captive to uncertainty, to chance, to fear and fate, and now someone tells you that this need not be, that you are a spiritual being and that you are as free as your thought and that wherever your confident thought can go, your body and your affairs will inevitably follow. If you respond to this, then you know your genealogy and you know your Father, and you can be admitted to the company of the free. If you still believe that events are thrust upon you willy-nilly, that you are the victim of cruel circumstances beyond your control, then you do not know your Father and you cannot get into Jerusalem, the City of Peace. But you *do* know that your Father is spirit and that spirit is the only sovereign agency in this world, whether it be the spirit in a spirited horse or a blue ribbon dog or a confident and assured human being.

Part of me looks outward through the senses and reports danger and hardship. Another part looks inward and says that I am sired by God and therefore all things good and happy are my destiny. The senses report loss, trouble, a hard winter ahead and gloomy prospects. But the soul answers: I Am; nothing can be added to me and nothing taken away. I am sufficient at all times and in all places. Since my Father is God, I am not mean or miserable but I am noble and distinguished and full of promise.

Notice what happens when you think from this point of view. All the old ugly emotions and fearful anxieties tend to put their tails between their legs and slink away into the shadows. Confidence and peace and equanimity return. The fires of joy and enthusiasm are rekindled upon the altar of the heart and all the juices of life begin to flow again. This is the prime source of the good emotions. Coming back in thought and reflection and concentration frequently and repetitively to this source is the one sure way of supplanting the troublesome emotions with good ones. For if one manages his feelings, he will manage his world.

So much is said today about harmful emotion that many regard strong feelings as a bad thing. They try to be unemotional, to hold back, to make no response to life's circumstances. They think perhaps it is childish or immature to express, and to be mature and civilized is to be reserved and immobile. Nothing could be more wrong. For to choke off the feelings is to choke off life. We move by feelings, by all the feelings. Even hate and anger may be useful at times if directed properly. For we can hate injustice, ignorance, indolence, greed and cruelty, and this is right. But to hate people is wrong, for people are not the source of our happiness or our misery. A person who does not know what to hate does not know what to love, and if he does not know what to love he is cut off from his source and so he cannot replenish his life with the health-giving emotions. Essentially, our whole life experience is a feeling thing. Any event or situation is what we feel it to be. Everything reduces at last to what we feel about it. We can be hurt or be pleased. We can love or hate, be assured or fearful; and if there is not insight or point of control, then we are the victims of our moods and mere flotsam and jetsam upon the ocean of life.

As an example of how anger is properly expressed, think of Eddie Rickenbacker lying in a hospital oxygen tent. He heard the radio announce that he was dying. To a man who had faced death on many other occasions and in many other circumstances and had taken its measure, this announcement was infuriating. He tore up the tent, threw a pitcher at the radio and got well. Emotion is power. It is good to express it but always and only in Divine Order. Divine Order means that anger must be directed not at people but rather at the small and sniveling thought which would depress the divinity in man, which would exalt things and circumstances above the spirit of man. Direct your anger at ignorance, at the suggestion of inferiority or weakness, at any thought or comment which would elevate the material world above the spiritual world. It will open up the inner gates of life and let the surging, unexpressed sovereignty come through and take charge. Emotional sovereignty is a great and wonderful thing and we can all have more of it by following this ancient rule of going back to the source and remembering who our true Father is and then allowing the mind to make its confident and consoling conclusion that because it comes from a high and noble source, it is endowed and equipped with more than enough to win the battles of this life.

Happiness Is a Game

HAPPINESS IS A GAME. Truth and error are the players. You are the umpire. Truth is God's thought in your mind of freedom and health. Truth tries to destroy the error. Error is man's ignorance or false belief which tries to overcome the Truth.

When you listen to any suggestion of sickness, weakness or failure, error has gotten in a good swat.

Then give your affairs a spiritual treatment. That is, begin to think about them from the standpoint of Truth rather than from the standpiont of man's false opinions. Recall that consciousness and not things is the cause of your experience. Error bases its belief on the power of things and conditions, so error is bound to lose. To be a winner in a game you must be alert to take advantage of the opponent's weak points. Do this with any and all suggestions of limitation. When error suggests that something will cause you hurt, remember that suggestion is false— that only your thought has power over you and *God is in your thought of good.*

Truth is a relaxed player. It plays for the fun of the game, never so serious as to be strained or anxious. Truth is never concerned about the outcome. God never fails.

Time, Life and Money

I WISH TO ADDRESS three things here: Time, Life, and Money; and I shall treat them as though they were nearly synonymous. If they are not precisely synonymous, they are at least one in substance and nature. Who has not heard that time is money and that time is the wise man's treasure? And whose reflection has not revealed to him that where there is no time there is no life, and where there is no life there is no time? For time is not an objective thing. It is not something that you can handle with your hands. Time is a mental sensation of events. Time is always associated with space, and that is why the scientist nowadays speaks of space-time. For example, when I left my home a few minutes ago, I entered a taxi and rode through traffic and stopped at lights and moved again and saw people and vehicles and buildings. I passed the time of day with acquaintances and finally entered the studio and began my radio broadcast. More than forty-five minutes had elapsed by my watch since I left home.

All these events give me the sensation of time. It is now nearly ten minutes of seven. What does that mean? The position of the hands on a clock or a watch, the position of the sun in the sky? Yes, but it means more. It illustrates how we take note of time only by its loss or its passing. We seem to be moving forward and time receding. When we reflect on this, we find it full of illusions. Time is different to different people. It is different to each of us at different periods. When we are sad, time is slow; when we are glad, time is mad. How time drags when you are waiting for something or someone! How fast it goes when you are busy! When we are joyful and interested, an hour is like a minute—and in grief, a minute is an eternity.

But before I go further with these abstractions, I want to tell a little fanciful story, whose source I do not know. A man had a dream and in that dream he came to a beautiful building like a bank. A sign on the front of the building said, Time for Sale. The dreamer saw a man breathless and pale painfully pull himself up the stairs like a sick man. The dreamer says, "I heard him say, 'The doctor told me I was five years too late in going to see him. I shall buy those five years now and he can save my life.'" The dreamer continues:

"Then came another, older, and spoke to the clerk in the big building: 'When it was too late, I discovered that God had given me great capacities and endowments and I failed to develop them. Sell me ten years so that I can be the man I could have been.'

"Then came a younger man and said: 'The company has told me that starting next month I can have a big job if I am prepared to take it. But I am not prepared. Sell me two years so that I will be ready to take the job next month.'

"So they came—ill, hopeless, despondent, worried, unhappy —and they left smiling, each man with a look of unutterable pleasure on his face, for he had what he so desperately needed: time.

"Then I awoke, glad that I had what these had not and what they could never buy: time to think and do what I want to do and what I must do. I hummed at my work that day; great happiness filled my heart—for I had time.''

The story points up what we all know but perhaps don't think about often enough: all we have is time, and time is life and time is money. All that was ever ours is ours now—time. Time is often painted as bald behind, with a lock of hair in front—to indicate that you have to catch him from in front: when he is gone, there is nothing to get hold of.

And all of this shows us that time is a thing of consciousness, not a fixed absolute, not a commodity that you buy or acquire, but a thing of the mind, a sensation of living and moving and experiencing. Time is what we all have in common, and each of us has exactly the same amount; and what we do with this single element determines all else about us. The kind of thinking that each of us is doing in this hour will be revealed in the next hour and in many hours that follow that. The only way to modify the hours of the future is to lay hold of the availability of this one. Control of the future is in our hands now, through proper use of the present. The only answer to the question What shall we do tomorrow? is to be found in what we are doing now. The only way to be happy tomorrow is to be happy today. But how? By laying fast hold upon this fundamental realization: that the only creative power is consciousness, and consciousness is this moment of awareness.

That is why the Master Teacher announced, ''I am the way, the life and the truth.'' That is, consciousness is the way, the life, and the truth. What is the way to health? It is through constructive attitudes and good feeling. If bad feeling does not invest the present, it cannot ever come into the future. In this day of psychosomatic medicine, everybody understands how bad feelings can make bad health and good feelings will maintain good health. So the truth as Jesus taught it remains: I am my health, my health is what I am. Each person is a way in himself.

The sum total of attitudes and beliefs and feelings constitutes not only the character of the person but the way in which he goes in life. An angry person is a person on the way to trouble. A composed person is a person on the way to good relations with others.

So I am the way and I am also life. What is the life of any one of us but his consciousness or the sum total of his feelings, sensations and attitudes? If we change these, we change the life. If for any brief moment we change a sad person's immediate consciousness by a humorous story or a diverting experience, we have changed his life for that moment. For his life is just exactly what he feels at that moment. Each one lives in his ideas and his beliefs, and if one has good ideas and noble thoughts and courageous feelings and hopeful attitudes then he is more alive than one who has not these. The person whose mind is full of resentment or bitterness or hopelessness or despair or fear is not really living. He is existing in a sort of half-death. In the case of the first person, time is blissful. His hours pass peacefully and happily and without any sense of burden. He tends to live long and richly because he invests every hour with some useful or amusing or inspiring attitude or reaction. By contrast, the hours of the other person are long, and life is a burden no matter how many years he lives. Time is heavy to him for he is not in a state of enjoyment.

Finally, the last part of this three-part statement is "I am the Truth." What is the truth or meaning to the individual of any situation but his individual viewpoint or belief or awareness or feeling about it at that particular time? The old story of the blind men and the elephant comes to mind. One blind man felt the side of the elephant and said the elephant is like a wall. Another felt the ear and said the elephant is like a fan. A third felt the leg of the elephant and said the elephant is like a post or a tree. Each was right and all were right. A hypnotized man can be constrained to see a dog which is not there or to see an apple when handed a lemon. Each person experiences life filtered through his viewpoint or opinion or conditioning. There is always a divine norm or a universal truth above and beyond individual opinions, but for all practical purposes each man experiences his own truth as his personal consciousness allows. So again we read and hear and understand that "I am the way, the truth and the life"—no manifestation cometh unto me except the Father or the source of all things or consciousness send him. And consciousness is this present awareness—this moment of time, this gap between two eternities, past and future. It is not only time, it is life and it is money, or it is production or it is manifestation and results and achievement.

What we do in consciousness we shall do in fact, and where we go in thought we shall travel with our feet, and what we engage with our mind we shall handle with our hands. This is the simple but profound truth. Knowing this, why should we be afraid of people or things or situations or any kind of external happening? Why should we be troubled or irritated with others? They are not the causes of our misery or our happiness. Only what we believe in our heart governs our future. Then why should we not, each of us and all of us, be as healthy as we can conceive, as happy as our mind can reach and as productive and wealthy as our belief can measure? The essence and the substance and the life of each of these desired goals is in the attitude and the mood with which we now regard them in this moment of time. So time is life and money and every other good; and so long as we are alive, time is available. New opportunities are ever returning to compensate for lost ones. Sarah can give birth at the age of ninety, and "I will restore unto you the years that the locusts have eaten." If you believe, all things are possible, for your belief is the essence of time.

The Safe Place
within Yourself

A PROMINENT AUTO-MAKER who is responsible for the expenditure of millions of dollars in new tools and dies for new models recently affirmed this: "I believe in a power greater than myself and a wisdom greater than my own. This power takes care of us when we try to do right. So I try to do right—just plain right. I may get tense but I don't worry, neither regarding my business, my family, my health, my stockholders or our employees or about my spiritual estate."

The auto-maker was telling this to a younger executive whom he was instructing in the ways of big business. The older man continued: "I just try to do right, whether it is designing a new car to cost millions to market or it is making up my mind whether to send a letter by air mail or by ordinary postage. Having decided, I don't worry. I leave results to Him. It may be childlike, I'll admit, but I think it's the smartest thing one can do. First, it takes a load off my shoulders, and second, it sets my mind free to think accurately and clearly. Third, it makes me able to enjoy recreation as well as work. Fourth, it makes me a human being instead of a mere machine, both in office and home. I think I'll last longer than if I, well, tried to run things by myself.''

Here is the simple and honest testimony of a successful and practical person. This man has made a working principle of a great and fundamental truth. It is fundamental to all religions. It is basic. Emerson suggests that we should get our ''bloated nothingness'' out of the way so that something bigger can pass through us. This is the secret of getting along in life, of being successful in what you are doing, of being happy in your environment. Until a man comes to the recognition of this Higher Power and allows it to work through him and with him, he tends to struggle with his environment and to fight with suppositional evils. He becomes a man of war, just as we read in the Bible that David became a man of war. At first he was a shepherd which, in the Bible, is the figure for the type of mind that is nonviolent and inoffensive. Then he became a man of war, fighting and resisting and opposing, just as we all do at some time or point in our lives.

But David found a better way, as we all must do. He came to a realization of the Life Principle, the One Power and the basic Law of Life. Then he went to war no more. For then there was nothing to fight. When man realizes his oneness with an Infinite Power whose will is good and whose works are right, that there is only One, and he, the individual, in agreement with that One, *is* that One, then there is nothing to oppose and nothing to oppose him. He has come into union with the All. And union with the All is union with all of its parts. That means that the person who has realized his union with the Infinite has found himself, his true self. He has a sense of the One being everywhere. All other people are but extensions and variations of himself. His environment and its processes and movements and changes are but the projections of his consciousness. All forms of life from the lowliest insect and worm on up are but levels of the single consciousness of the universe. There is no need to hate, to grow angry, to fight and to oppose; there is need only to know and to realize the Truth. As the old motto used to have it:

> You do not need to fight,
> You do not need to struggle,
> You only have to know.

It is a wonderful and splendid thing to see what happens to a person when the Higher Will operates through him; when, as Emerson suggests, he gives passage to the beams of a higher light than his own. When he acts manfully and resists not. It is no position of weakness and retreat as some might at first suppose. It is, on the contrary, a position of impregnable strength, for this kind of person wins his ends and he wins them without the expenditure of great energy and time and effort. A sort of effortlessness creeps through all of his operations. This does not put any premium on laziness but it does make all labor easier. The whole evolutionary process of life seems to be leading each individual to this realization. Religion, in general, has always referred to this realization as the worship of God. So often a person's worship of God is merely the fear of a power he does not understand and he attempts by prayer and religious exercises to placate that power and to cause it to forgive his sins and bless his operations. It is primitive, to say the least. With the person of spiritual insight, however, worship of God simply means his active realization of a higher power's wisdom working through him and through all men and all things constantly and forever. To worship means to count worthy and to place first. It means to have a proper sense of values, a proper estimate of what is first and fundamental.

We do not need to be reminded that millions of us are unsafe and insecure, anxious and depressed, but we *do* need to be made to realize that millions are this way because they have no contact with the central Truth. They have lost their attachment with the Universal and they cannot continue their life until the attachment is made again. A person who has made this attachment, who has established his unity with the One, is secure. He runs no more and he fights no more. He has found the base. He has "transferred the burden," just as the auto-maker indicates he has "transferred the burden," though, in a human way of speaking, he carries tremendous loads. One great industrialist, of whom I have spoken recently, heads up worldwide enterprises that, all told, employ thirty million people. Think of the responsibilities that rest upon the shoulders of this man, humanly speaking! His decisions are literally directing the lives and fortunes of thirty million people. If his decisions are good, these people prosper. If his decisions are bad, they suffer. (Spiritually speaking, of course, every individual has the freedom and the power to determine his own destiny by his own individual consciousness of good.) Humanly speaking, one would say that this man must go to bed with a tremendous load but that is not so. He has learned to divest himself of the burden, to transfer it to a Higher Mind which he believes speaks through him and aids him and guides in his decisions, and so it does.

But one is not secure merely because he realizes this One Power and is willing for it to work through him. One must be willing to risk everything else in defense of this position. That is what it means to put first, or to worship. I. A. R. Wiley tells of walking by a deep and frozen canal one winter day with her little dog, Susie. Suddenly Susie shot out across the ice in pursuit of some imaginary quarry. The ice broke under her weight and she began to drown in the frigid water, being unable to regain her footing on the ice. The famous author says, "I knew I had no choice; I went in up to my chin and then with a final plunge, got hold of the dog and brought her out." It was a five mile drive back and though her clothes were frozen on her she did not feel cold nor did she get sick from the immersion. "I was exhilarated and happy as never before. I have never lost what that incident bequeathed to me—that I can and will risk my life, and that after all, I am not so terribly afraid of death or anything. To that extent I have become safe. I know, on the other hand, that had I left my puppy to drown, I would never be safe again.''

There is only one safe place and it is within, where one lives with one's own conscience, with one's character and one's convictions and has all of these based upon the sure foundation of the realization of God. One cannot give mere lip service or announce his faith as a mere creed of words or even as a mere form or rite. The safe place within is a matter of inner consciousness and conviction and it is this only when we are willing to risk it. If you announce that you have faith and then promptly you doubt, it is evident that you did not have faith. Faith is an immovable conviction which in the face of all sorts of discouraging evidence still stands firm and unmoved, and the real test of this is some set of discouraging circumstances, some threat from without, some adventure, some test in which we put our faith on the table and win. Spiritually we must consider ourselves as having real faith. We are endowed. We are equipped and our best equipment is the realization of our union with the whole. This is at once our own individual enfranchisement and strength and power and ability and also our security and peace. Then Christ, or the God-Self, is born in us.

Burn Your Bridges

BURN YOUR BRIDGES behind you. Admit no thought of the possibility of retreat. There is no going back. The only way is forward. Having seen and declared your objective, move toward it. Never take your eyes from it. You must mentally possess it and act as though it were accomplished even while your feet are on the way to it. You must *be* before you can *have*.

The young girl who marries with the thought "I can always go back to mother" is leaving a bridge on which to retreat. Her marital adventure is headed for trouble before it begins. Bridges are to be used. If you leave them in the mind the mind will use them. The man who is always planning "outs" or leaving a way of escape or devising a face-saver "just in case" is sabotaging his own success.

For individual or for nation there is no road back. The lesson of the ages is "swim or sink," "do or die," but don't retreat. It is always farther back. The other shore is closer than you think.

The Law of Healthy-Mindedness

WALT WHITMAN SAYS: "I am sufficient as I am." This is healthy-mindedness. It brings rest and peace to the mind. It precludes that feverish straining and striving after something which seems to be outside one's self. This statement of Whitman's is the recognition of basic wholeness and an acceptance of it. The soul contains all things. It is an infinity of possibilities. The Good Gray Poet, as Whitman is called, sounded this note of adequacy and basic wholeness in other inspiring and triumphant phrases, such as "I did not know I was so large" . . . "I am large, I contain multitudes" . . . "I have slumbered upon myself too long." Whatever else the realization of this great truth may do to one, it will at the very least carry his mind back to contact with the basic wholeness and strength and sustenance, which will tend in every way to heal his mind, his body and his affairs.

One of the great sources of trouble in our modern age is the fact that many of the old religious concepts and doctrines have lost validity for many people and are no longer a source of strength. Man today is like a child lost from his parents in a vast crowd. He seeks vainly for his parent's hand or the sound of his parent's voice, but is met on every hand by strange forms, strange sounds and strange sights. Nothing could be more helpful, more comforting, more healing to him, than to hear the sound of a familiar voice and to have a familiar hand grasp his own. Wherever religion is valid it is so because it helps people to get in touch with the basic wholeness of life and to maintain communion with it.

But every person can't, or at least doesn't, accept his basic wholeness. And because wholeness is not accepted, inferiority and weakness are felt, and people become like children, afraid of the dark, afraid of loud noises and of strange sounds and sights. When children are hurt or frightened they run to their parents to be assured that everything is all right. That is what we all want to know whether we realize it or not—that everything is all right, that we are secure, that wholeness and adequacy attend us on every hand. When one is sick, it helps especially to think this and to realize it. And one is sick until he can think and realize this.

Let me put all this into psychological terms and give another dimension to our view of the mind's function in regard to basic wholeness. One of the basic laws of the mind is this: "The subconscious mind is amenable to suggestion." This means that the subconscious mind does not reason and think things out for itself as does the conscious mind. It does not make comparisons and contrasts. It never questions about good or evil. It does not choose one thing or course of action in preference to another. It simply reacts to the impressions that are given it by the conscious mind. It expresses its impressions. Phineas P. Quimby, the famous healer and psychoanalyst, said, "Man acts as he is acted upon." He explains that man is acted upon by ideas and he reacts in accordance with the impressions these ideas make upon him. If you will think about this it will be obvious that two different people will react to the same suggestion in two different ways. Therefore the suggestion is not absolute in its influence. A suggestion does not impose a force from without, but only opens a door whence a smaller or greater amount of the basic wholeness of life can escape into expression with the suggestion. If the suggestion is of harm, it does not mean that harm is on the inside of the individual, as a constituent part of his being; it means that the suggestion opens a small door through which only a small part of the basic wholeness can emerge. Pain and misery and suffering of all kinds are due not to the activity of a power apart from ourselves, or the imposition of any evil from without, but rather to the partial experience of our own wholeness. A friend of mine who is ninety-five met a man on the street the other day who is sixty-five. Complained the man of sixty-five, "I am losing my memory." Said the man of ninety-five, "You can't lose memory, you are not using what memory you have. If I tie your right hand to your breast and keep it there for several months, you will lose the use of your hand and arm. My memory," he said, "is as good as it ever was. I do not believe in loss of memory."

It is our beliefs and our opinions, so many of them gained from hearsay and from limited race experience, that act as inhibitors upon the basic wholeness of our nature and which open only small apertures through which the imprisoned splendor may escape into expression. To illustrate how minds are conditioned to think in narrow, limited fashion, here is an account of an experiment which was conducted at Swarthmore College: a professor of psychology brought his students into a room where a rusty iron pipe was mounted upright on the table, and inside the pipe was a pingpong ball at the bottom. The professor told the students that the problem they had to solve was to get the pingpong ball out of the pipe. In the room were these articles: a hammer, pliers, rulers, soda straws, pens and a bucket full of dirty wash water. The students began by fishing around vainly with the various tools. Finally about one half of them saw that the solution lay in pouring the dirty water into the pipe and floating the ball to the top.

Then the professor repeated the experiment with another group of students, but with one difference. Instead of the bucket of dirty water, he placed a pitcher of ice water on a crisp, clean cloth surrounded by gleaming goblets. Not one student solved the problem!

Do you doubt then that suggestion rules and governs our mental operations and therefore our experiences? Can you doubt how suggestion operates by limiting the flow of the basic wholeness which we are, by filling the mind with inhibitory influences? These inhibitors, I say again, do not bring harm to the mind; they only limit the passage of the good which is always available to every one of us. The evil power in the world is not a power in and of itself, having intelligence and initiative and will; it is only a denial of the good power. The devil's language is ''No.''

Many ways have been discovered to analyze the mind and find what the inhibitors are. Most modern psychological emphasis has been placed upon locating and isolating these inhibiting factors. This is undoubtedly helpful for a lot of people who are not on the spiritual basis, but for those who can get on the spiritual basis quickly it is unnecessary. Paul tells us in the eighth chapter of Romans that, ''To be spiritually minded is life and peace.'' That is, to have in the mind and before the mind, not merely suggestions of life and peace, but to think from a spiritual basis as Whitman does when he says, ''I am sufficient as I am.'' This recognition of the basic wholeness and the inner splendor of a man, when enthroned as the regnant Lord of the Mind, becomes a door wide enough through which the basic wholeness can pour into objective expression in the individual life. This enthronement of Truth in the mind is represented by the coming of Jesus to the impotent man at the pool at Bethesda and telling him to get on his feet. It takes no account of the inhibiting factors complained of. These inhibitors are canceled and made impotent themselves, and potency leads impotency captive. No need to analyze and isolate here. The one great Truth has canceled and made inoperative all the untruths. If you know your immunity to seasickness, all the suggestions in the world to the contrary will have no harmful effect, but rather will be turned to good account in your behalf; for every suggestion of seasickness will only arouse your confidence.

The majority of mankind is still primitive in its religion. It puts power in things and forces outside of itself. As the primitives located gods in rocks, trees, streams, clouds and all external phenomena, so does the primitive mind in modern times locate the powers of health and sickness, of happiness and failure, in things and situations outside of itself. Such a modern mind is not much better off, if at all, than the ancient primitive mind which peopled the outside world with demons and angels, for then and now such a mind neglects the spiritual truth that all things are within itself and that to look within is the first lesson in the spiritual life.

In the Bible the understanding is that flesh is form and that form is external and secondary, and has no power in and of itself. Therefore to put trust or fear in it is a mistake. But to remember the inner splendor and to think, "I am sufficient as I am" and to think of the Infinite Majesty behind one's personality and supporting it, which is our very self behind the facade of our person, and to think of the adequacy that this gives us and to rejoice in this—this is spiritual-mindedness, or, in our phrase, healthy-mindedness. In other words, "He who discovers himself loses his misery."

What Is Right
with You?

MY FRIEND THE LATE Don Blanding, the poet from
Hawaii, once greeted a friend on a California street with the remark, "Before you tell me what is wrong, tell me what is right
with you." The friend, a woman, was completely baffled. It was
an approach she had not expected. It suggested a way of thinking which she had long ago forgotten. For Don Blanding knew
her history and her personality traits and tendencies. Had he
asked her How is your health? he would have gotten a long
description about her sufferings, though they were all exagger-
ated and he knew her to be in very good health generally. But
a person who gets into the habit of complaining always manages
to find plenty to complain about. One person, for example, who
is perfectly healthy will answer that inquiry by replying, "That
is just the trouble. Just because I am as strong as an ox, I am always asked to do things, while those frail, fluttery women get
all of the waiting upon." This woman had good eyesight and had
a good job, too, but if you had asked her about either one of them
you would have heard a list of complaints. To the first she would

43

have replied complainingly, ''Because I have good eyes, I have to read the newspapers to my father, who has poor eyes.'' If you persisted and said, ''But you do have a good job,'' she would have replied, ''Yes, but don't expect me to be grateful for that. I work for my living; all my sisters have husbands to support them.'' Perhaps you know someone like this. But be careful and don't look too far from home. We can all find such a person at times very close to home. The ungrateful, complaining attitude can become a vice and vices always destroy. It can become a self-made hell in which one burns, on fire with his own misery. André Maurois, the French writer, said that ''Life is too short to be little.'' We may add that life is little whenever we think too long on little things. The little worries and trivialities and the little grievances and complaints are like the Lilliputians, the little people who gradually bind the giant Gulliver, within ourselves because we are asleep and forgetful or indifferent to the truth of our being.

Judge Joseph Sabbath of Chicago acted as an arbitrator in forty to fifty thousand unhappy marriages. After listening to the griefs of over a hundred thousand battling wives and husbands, he lighted his pipe one afternoon and said: ''Trivialities are at the bottom of most marital unhappiness.'' What a commentary on marriage in particular and the human race in general this conclusion of the long-time Judge is! It is a sad fact that where minds are not anchored in the knowledge of the spiritual truth of being, they are unavoidably pulled apart and disintegrated by the sensations and trivialities of the outer world. Human emotions, in the Bible, for example, are often compared to a herd of cattle or sheep and the mind is the shepherd. If the mind goes to sleep or is unaware or is indifferent or is deluded, then the sheep are scattered. For our emotions are like sheep which need to be herded and shepherded and protected. I ought to say that the good emotions are like sheep, for the bad emotions are like the wolves which tear the sheep apart and scatter them. It is the duty of the enlightened mind to shepherd its sheep and keep the wolves away.

Take that wonderful pair, Gilbert and Sullivan of the marvelous Gilbert and Sullivan operettas. Gilbert wrote the delightful but zany lyrics and Sullivan wrote the enchanting music. Together, they had no peer, but they, too, fell apart over trivialities. They bought their own theater and Sullivan thought that it needed a new carpet so he ordered one. When Gilbert saw the bill he exploded. They battled it out in court and never spoke to each other again. As long as they lived they had no conversation with each other. Thereafter in their collaboration, whenever Sullivan wrote some music he mailed it to Gilbert and when Gilbert wrote some words he mailed them to Sullivan. Tragic isn't it, when you think of these two giants of art in the theater acting like children. It is the little things like this that ruin more people than the big troubles of life. The little worries and complaints and misunderstandings divide the forces of the mind, split it up and scatter the emotions of faith and confidence and assurance and goodwill.

Out on a slope in the Colorado mountains there lies the ruin of a gigantic tree. Naturalists say that that tree stood for over four hundred years. It was a seedling when Columbus came to this hemisphere. Lightning struck it over fourteen times. Avalanches and the storms of four centuries buffeted it but it survived them all. In the end, an army of beetles attacked it. They ate through the bark to the heart of the tree and sent it to the ground. Thus, the giant was felled by tiny little things.

There is a cure for thinking little, of course. It is to think big. In order to think big you must have something big to think about. The worried, fretful, complaining mind is usually thinking about details and trivialities outside of itself. Its path is discursive and erratic, running first from one thing to another. It must learn sometime to come home to itself, and as the Scripture says, "Be still and know that I am God." You and I are not the result of our effort and work and circumstances so much as we are the product of our meditations. "As a man thinketh in his heart, so is he." What you come back to most often in your mind when you are alone and think upon and accept, this becomes your destiny and your fate. There is no escape from this law. But if you should follow the psalmist and "Be still and know that I am God" and continue to meditate on this frequently, there will come a time when your own mind is no longer saying the words but something vast and infinite is taking up the meditation and thinking in you. Surely at that time you will feel a vastness and an infinity and a greatness about your being which will transcend all of your littleness. Thereafter you will think better of yourself for you will estimate yourself not it terms of your old habits and attitudes but in terms of a new and larger dimension which has been born out of your meditation.

Moreover, when this new center is established in the mind and heart as an anchor for the thinking, it automatically disperses the trivialities of life and makes them what they truly are, trivial and unworthy of more than a moment's attention. That is why in the Old Testament book of Leviticus it says, "He shall chase your enemies and they shall fall before you by the sword." This does not mean the literal sword of course and it does not mean literal enemies. When one is complaining and fretting and stewing, who are his enemies? Are they not the little trivialities of life which he is allowing his mind to magnify out of all proportion? His wrong attitudes toward these are his real enemies and his enlightened reason is the sword which will chase them. This passage continues in the twenty-sixth chapter with these words: "And five of you shall chase an hundred, and an hundred of you shall put ten thousand to flight: and your enemies shall fall before you by the sword." What does it mean when it says that five of you shall chase an hundred? Surely there are five parts to our mind—the five senses with which we all are acquainted. Take, as an example, the eyes and ears alone. They bring us reports of many things which disturb us and if we do not know better we are led forth into fear or anxiety or anger by the reports the eyes and ears bring to us. But if we meditated long upon the true center of our being, then we know that it is not what happens outside of us that makes our fate or our destiny or our experience, but rather what happens inside of us in the form of our attitudes toward circumstances.

If we know this, we do not lend so much credence or give so much importance to the reports of the senses. So it is a cloudy day; what of it? Since all things are changing, the sun will shine within a few hours. It is inevitable. So you failed in what you undertook. All is not lost. One failure does not constitute defeat. In fact, failure suggests effort and aspiration, for one who is not failing now and then is not attempting anything new. So, by thinking in these ways one disciplines the five senses and does not allow them to rove all over the world fearing this, growing anxious at that, being concerned with the other, but curbs them and makes them stay at home in a center of peace and thus the Scripture says, ''five of you shall chase an hundred''—shall chase the hundred sensations and appearances and happenings that come to the mind every hour and let them go on by instead of stopping them and being attentive to them and inviting them into the house of the mind, where they create only confusion and warfare.

If you have ever been restless or sleepless at night, you will remember that you wakened or you stayed awake because a whole stream of images and thoughts and old bits of conversations, perhaps a song or two, were running through your mind and occupying your attention, keeping you awake. Events of the preceding day or days were reliving themselves in your imagery and prospects and contemplations of the activities to come kept presenting themselves for consideration. You know that you slept only when you were able to drop all of these images and memories and thoughts from the mind and sink into your own center and close the door. Only when you became indifferent did these flocks of images cease to press in upon you and instead evaporated and left you alone. Something similar happens when we study and apply the divine science to our daily life. We learn to rethink our position in connection with the many trivialities and small anxieties that trouble the unschooled mind. Instead of following them attentively and obediently as though we had to, we stop and think about something else—a larger fact, a greater truth, such as the psalmist's words "Be still and know that I am God."

Get the attention fixed upon the Great Self which you eternally are, no matter what your human history with its foibles and mistakes and shortcomings, and the mind will get still and satisfied, and, as Elizabeth Barrett Browning is credited with saying, "The little cares which fretted me, I lost them yesterday . . . the foolish fears of what may happen, I cast them all away, among the clover-scented grass, among the new-mown hay; among the rustling of the corn, where drowsy poppies nod, where ill thoughts die and good are born—out in the fields with God." Only you don't have to go to the fields to do it. Find any great truth which inspires you and then meditate upon that. Do it again and again and your wayward mind will no longer deal in trivialities nor stoop to little things. There is a way to peace in this changing world and all of the sages of the ages have taught it. As Moses says, it is not up in the sky nor down in the earth that you must go to fetch it; rather it is in your mouth and in your hand—that is, in your speech and in your practice.

Things Don't Happen

THERE IS A CAUSE for everything! Nothing ever "just happens." What man calls "luck" or "chance" is only another name for his ignorance of the cause. To speak simply, the cause of anything in your world is the mood in which you dwell. Your habitual feeling about yourself and your world will translate itself into its physical image and likeness. The cause, therefore, is always within you, never without.

Spirit is God, the Creator. The particular spirit that animates you at any time is the way God is working in your life. If you are fearful, you have the spirit of fear and that means that you are creating more things to fear. If you are full of courage and faith regarding your objectives, you have a mood or spirit that will demonstrate. Such a spirit means that God in you is creating more things of satisfaction and joy in your life. Nothing is impossible to such a spirit. It will cross rivers and move mountains. It is scientific and you can bank on it and see results.

"Things don't happen. They are pushed from behind."
—Emerson

Why Doesn't God?

ANONYMOUS LETTERS are not usually very helpful but I recall one I received after President Kennedy's death. The writer said, "Since his death, I realize that I have lost faith in religion and all sermons and talks on religion." Then he or she (and I suspect it is a she) goes on to say that "A mighty oak is leveled by borers; a mansion can be laid low by termites, and floods and fires take the lives of thousands; ships and planes go down and there must be those aboard who have faith, but they all go down, good and bad together . . . I really believe religion isn't getting over to people and has let us down."

A first reaction to the letter is sympathy, then pity, then fear for the writer, but finally a relieved smile at the realization that the writer is playing a little game with herself and with others. At first one thinks, How can such a person be so discouraged and depressed about life and continue to live? If one feels so depressed by the cruelties of life, has lost faith in all religion and idealism, sees no prospect that pleases, and insists upon the gloomy outlook, then why stick around? There are a vast number of people like this in the world who enjoy pointing out all of the cruelties and sorrows and tragedies of life, as an argument against the efficacy of faith. One would think that they were quite unhappy souls, but this is not true. Quite the contrary. They enjoy what they are doing. They have a kind of enthusiasm for their negative philosophy. And it is joy and enthusiasm that keep body and soul together.

This person is not unhappy; she was trying to make me unhappy. She was enjoying herself in developing the philosophy of what is called the devil's beatitude: "Blessed be nothing." That is typical of people who develop this philosophy. They are all gloom and discouragement on the outside but on the inside a certain secret and perverted enjoyment, mostly at the expense of other people, keeps them going in reasonably good fettle. We have all seen or experienced the person who keeps the rest of the family concerned and worried about him or her by always threatening to have a heart attack or by frequently speaking of "when I am gone." They gain a kind of emotional strangle-hold over the rest of the family through a misbegotten or unduly extended sympathy. They usually outlive the rest of the family.

It reminds me of a piece the late I. A. R. Wylie wrote called, "Are You a Grievance Collector?" My letter writer is a grievance collector. These people collect grievances as other people collect stamps or objects of art. They treasure their collection and get a certain secret pleasure from it. Miss Wylie, with her great perceptiveness into human nature recalls a cross-looking little girl sitting on the doorstep of a London backyard and glowering into space. It was her fourth birthday and her parents had forgotten it until late in the afternoon. They were preoccupied with the larger problem of how to meet the rent. She would not be comforted or made up to. She went to bed, hugging her grief. She would not admit it, but she was enjoying herself. She was the heroine in a tragedy, the forsaken, mistreated, sacrificial being. In her gloomy aloofness she was gaining an emotional strangle-hold over her parents, a hold that would cover her own transgressions for many a day. Of course that little girl was Miss

Wylie herself. The vivid memory of this early experience as a grievance collector helped her to work out of this grievance-collecting tendency and to understand it in others.

Children who learn grievance collecting too early in life grow up to be like the woman Miss Wylie described as living next door to her. A low wall divided their backyards. Over this wall the two women occasionally exchanged greetings and advice. Every comment Miss Wylie made was met with some bitter, nagging complaint. Either there was too much sun or the single tree in the Wylie yard was throwing too much shade on the other yard or the woman had been sold inferior bulbs or children and dogs were trampling her flower beds. Out of patience one day with all this, Miss Wylie said to her, "If you ever admitted that anything went right with you, I should fall in a dead faint." The neighbor never spoke to her again. She had been deprived of her one great satisfaction in life: her grievance against it. If the woman had really been intent upon real happiness she would have taken that remark with good grace and allowed it to challenge her immaturity and to call forth her maturity.

There is something in each of us that wants to enjoy a good wrong. And if it is indulged, we can easily fall into the habit of being a grievance collector. Such people collect grievances not only against other people but against life itself, against God and the universe. They say, "If God is love, why doesn't He cure the evil in the world? Why does He allow pain and all sorts of cruel misfortune? Why did He not make us without the tendency to think and to do evil? Why does He allow the appalling pain and bloodshed and sorrow and inhumanity? If He is all-powerful, why does He not stop all this?" These people also suggest that religion has failed, forgetting that religion is not something apart from a person that it can fail or succeed by itself. There can be, and often is, a vast difference between professed or nominal religion and the actual religon of the heart. Nominal religion is what a person is born into, subscribes to, or reads or professes. This is often largely theoretical and prospective. But a person's working religion is just what he thinks and how he feels not only about himself but about all other people and all other things and conditions in the world. Every religious person has a public religion and a private religion and the latter is the most meaningful. Sometimes the two agree; often they do not.

Religion does not fail; it is people who fail. All religions teach the Golden Rule, and this rule has never failed. But a person, while he assents to the Golden Rule with his mind, may not be tied to it in his feelings. Fear may move a person more than faith, in which case he has a religion of fear. Similarly people have a religion of hate or anger or confusion or gloom. So it may be said that every person in the world has some religion. He has some secret helm, as Emerson says, which he obeys, some god which he worships, some concept which governs him, some conviction which is an executive force in his life. "There be lords many and gods many," says Paul, "but we know one Lord." In other words, there are many concepts and beliefs which tie one into the creative power, but there is one creative power and that is consciousness alone.

Faith that falters because planes fail and ships sink and presidents are shot and tragedies of various kinds come to people is not faith, for true faith is not based upon events but rather upon the laws of the spirit and the unswerving conviction that consciousness alone is cause and that character is fate. True faith is not sustained by what happens or does not happen to people, but it is sustained by principles and insights and by the remembrance of the spiritual laws which are just as sure and just as accurate as the laws of matter.

People who ask, "Why doesn't God do something about all the suffering and the tragedy in the world?" forget that God is not a man. God is Cosmic Mind, Universal Intelligence and Infinite Will or Tendency. The Universal does not, because it cannot, deal with individual details. As Judge Troward has so well said, ''The Universal cannot act upon the plane of the particular without itself becoming the particular.'' And when it does that, it becomes a man. If God could act as a person, He would: prevent war, heal all the sick and diseased, establish peace and brotherhood and plenty over all the earth, and enforce the Golden Rule everywhere. But God cannot do these things except through and as man.

In still another sense, God has already done all of these things in principle. The works of mercy and redemption and healing and renewal always wait for the prepared mind, the understanding heart and the redirected will of man.

In the Bible these two poles of being are called the Father and the Son. We are directed to observe that ''the Son can do nothing of himself, but what he seeth the Father do; for what things soever he doeth, these also doeth the Son likewise.'' It is the province of the Father to generalize and to create cosmically, to establish great general principles; it is the province of the Son to observe those general principles and to apply them particularly. What distinguishes an Edison or a Marconi from the apprentice who can hook up an electric bell by rule of thumb? The former perceive the great general laws of electricity and bring them to particular application. Once observe and see and understand those general principles, and you can apply them in all sorts of labor-saving and comfort-producing situations.

The greater accomplishment always results from the greater seeing. How did men learn to fly? By watching the birds, principally. They observed the general principles of flight and applied them in local situations. The principles of flight were always subsistent in the nature of the universe around us, but it took minds capable of seeing and observing and of experimenting and of making large generalizations and then applying those generalizations to local and particular uses. Thus the Bible speaks scientifically when it says the Son can do nothing but what he sees the Father do and whatsoever he sees the Father doing, these things he doeth likewise.

Why doesn't God prevent the evil, heal the sick, protect the weak? The answer is that He has done all of these things and more already—in principle. The next step is for us to look at the Father and see the principle and then allow it to work locally in our own individual lives. God has already finished his work and it is all good. Man's work is in process. Let us see—and seeing, believe—and believing, trust—and trusting, receive *now* into our lives universal strength and power.

You Cannot Fail

You cannot fail if you know who you are. As a *human being*, you *can* fail.

As the *Son of God*, you are fated to *succeed*. The destiny of anything can only be the unfoldment of its own nature. You are Life and Life is God. To feel this strongly is to demonstrate it. The Law of Success is belief. Your humanness exists only in your limited belief about yourself. If you believe yourself to be human, finite, mortal, then you are subject to the destiny of the mortal which is extinction. Don't quibble by saying you are part human, part Divine. You are either all one or all the other. There are no divided Kingdoms in nature.

When you see yourself to be the presence of the One and Only Life or Being, you will know you are failure-proof. You are geared to the wheels of fortune. You are inextricably bound up in the plan and destiny of the universe. Your self opens out into a larger Self which is All. You can believe in God—for you are God in action.

Handling the
Ups and Downs

UPS AND DOWNS are common. We all have them. Most of us are aware that our emotions run in cycles and that very often we are the victim of our own emotional cycles. The average person takes it for granted that a run of bad luck will get him "down." Whereas, good news will take him "sky high."

Scientists who have studied the rise and fall of human emotion have pointed out that this is not true. They have found that emotional cycles are built into human beings. Dr. Rexford B. Hersey of the University of Pensylvania made this discovery many years ago. He found that with all of us high and low spirits follow each other with a regularity almost as dependable as that of the tides. External conditions merely advance or postpone our regular periods of elation or depression. Thus good news gives your spirits only a brief boost when you are in a low period and bad news is less depressing when you are in a high period. For example, one man lost his arm in an auto accident. It occurred during his "high" period. For the first few weeks at the hospital he remained quite cheerful. He joked about not being able to keep a good man down and offered the suggestion that,

"Maybe I'll get me a better job with one arm than I had with two."

It worked out just that way. When he returned to work he was made a minor supervisor. But by that time he was in a low period and became depressed instead of being elated. He broke off his engagement with a girl who was in love with him by explaining, "She is probably just feeling sorry for me."

The trouble with such studies and research projects is that they change the explanation of the condition but continue to confirm us in our weakness and extremity. Instead of outside conditions to blame for the rise and fall of our moods, they give us some inside conditions. The awful bondage of this may be seen in the scientists' recommendation to keep track of your emotional cycles so that you will know when to expect a high or low period. They suggest that one mark on the calendar the days when one is unusually depressed. Presumably, after you keep this up for a few weeks, you will know how many days or weeks it takes you to make a round trip from high to low and back to high again. Then, knowing when to expect your next low period, you plan your work accordingly. You save the rough jobs for your high period and try to coast along with an easy routine when you are in a low period.

This is the same old bondage with another name and explanation. Instead of blaming outside conditions for raising or lowering your spirits, now you blame a built-in pattern of which you are the victim. All opposite kinds of thinking which predicate health or illness, happiness or misery upon the turn of events, the turnings of the stars or the emotional cycles do but bind one in error, limitation and bondage. To find life and happiness and to avoid the miseries of the ups and downs, to avoid the extremes of up and down, one must align and square himself with the perfect law of consciousness.

Consider the lily. It has an innate capacity for living the perfect life of the lily. Consider the lily because it reminds us that plants and animals live a more perfect life in many ways than do human beings. They follow nature and nature's laws more accurately. The lily has a built-in intelligence within the seed or the bulb which functions in one way and in one way only and that is always affirmatively and constructively towards life. The lily is responsive by nature to the sun. The sun calls and the lily responds. The lily can do no other for it has no negative will.

Now the spiritual sun, or truth, calls all men but not all men respond, even as not all men respond to a good day and good weather. Speak of how fine and pleasant a morning it is and some minds will respond by saying, "It's a weather-breeder," or, "It will probably snow." In other words, man is negative as well as positive. He can use his thought in either of two ways. He can say, "Yes" to truth or he can say, "No." The lily and all things in nature are so constructed that they can say only "Yes" to truth, to right action and to positive, constructive impulses of growth. They have no negative will. But man is so constructed as to have freedom to enable him to have choice, to enable him to learn and to understand. Before he comes to understanding he is negative to the point that he expects to meet bad luck and expects to be unhappy and since the law of his life is "As a man thinketh in his heart, so is he," what man expects to be or to find, he becomes and he experiences.

This is all taught in the Bible but man does not yet know it to any great extent. We have had the teachings of Moses for thirty-five hundred years, the teachings of Isaiah for three thousand years and the teachings of Jesus for something less than two thousand years and yet we still make response to and bow down in obedience to the false gods of outside circumstances or conditioned patterns within. Man does not realize that it is his own thought that is bringing him his misery or his happiness and that to change the character and the nature of his thought is to change the character and the nature of his experience. Marking dates upon a calendar and noting the cyclic movement of one's emotion without also remembering that one's own spiritual will can change this cycle puts one in bondage to the cycle. Each time the dark mood comes, the individual feels that it has come upon him by means of another agency than his own will and so he subjects himself in his thought and becomes a suppliant, a slave.

This kind of thing goes on and on until a man puts two and two together and discovers the relationship between his thoughts and his experiences. This is a great day in the life of any individual for he has then arrived at understanding. Then he knows the true God as the I Am. In other words, consciousness, whether universal or individual, is the true creator of all phenomena and experience. "Have ye not known," asks the prophet Isaiah, "have ye not heard, have ye not understood from the foundation of the earth that it is He that sitteth on the circle of the earth?" (Isaiah 40:21).

When you yourself, if you have not already done so, reach this place of dynamic understanding and realization, you will cease to think negatively. You will have awareness and light and that light will redeem your world. This will give you back your spiritual will and you will respond to the pull of the spiritual sun bidding you to move towards life and happiness as does the lily.

Surely this is what Jesus means us to consider when He asks us to "Consider the lily." The lily and other things in nature living under the blanket law of nature do this "by nature." They are made to do what is right and good for them. But you and I as human beings are made with a free will. We can move affirmatively or we can move negatively. This is for the purpose of putting two and two together and learning the effect of our thought and our choice, so that gradually we learn to move affirmatively by becoming aware of the consequences of moving negatively. It is then that we have arrived at a self-conscious knowledge of that truth and that principle which is automatic and subconscious in the pine tree and the lily and other forms of nature. In other words, you and I have to do what the lily does but do it consciously in the face of powerful suggestion and opposition to the contrary. That is why the Master told us to "Judge not by appearances, but judge righteous judgment." That is, move constructively with force and power and will and initiative. The principle of life will honor our will and our initiative and give us what we seek. The victory that comes from this self-discovery is the knowledge of the kingdom of heaven which is within us. Then we worry about trivia and details no more for we have found ourselves and we have found life. Knowing the principle of the spiritual will, the principle of self-action and independence, we no longer give the power of changing our emotions to circumstances and conditions outside of us. We learn to say with the apostle, "None of these things moves me." No more do we give power to old habits and patterns and conditionings within the self, within the personality, for we know that these too yield and change under the power of an enlightened will. Think deeply within yourself that "Like the lily, I have one purpose, one will and one way to go and that is forward into life in divine law and order. All things and persons everywhere are constrained by the law of life to cooperate with me in this and none can do me wrong. Even those who ignorantly seek to hurt or to delay me will be constrained by the law of life to help and to bless me."

The One Remedy

IT WOULD BE a rather wonderful thing, don't you think, if there were a single remedy for all of our ills and tribulations. Men have always thought there was as evidenced by their continual search for panaceas and cure-alls and fountains of youth. The search still goes on too, like the search for the cure of the common cold.

Many of us will undoubtedly remember and all of us have heard of the old-time medicine man who used to go through the country peddling his remedy—and usually he had just one remedy, which was good for practically everything. It was, in other words, a cure-all—good for falling hair, fallen arches, heart trouble or the itch. Moreover, it was good for man or beast— take it and get well of anything that bothered you. We laugh at such things now. We believe we live in a more scientific age and indeed we do. But the amazing thing about the medicine-peddler was that his remedy worked so well. It probably would not be quite so effective today, for fewer people would believe in it.

That is the point of this essay: that anything which engenders your belief and confidence will do you good. Actually, it is not the thing nor the substance but the belief that does the good. Wherefore we have it written as a law in our Scriptures that everything is done unto us according to our belief. Or, in other words, "According to your faith, so be it done unto you." The medicine itself, which was peddled by the old-time medicine man, probably had very little value except as a means for the sufferer to believe that he would get well. It was a ladder for his faith and as such it was very good. The stuff which the peddler sold was good for nearly every trouble. Indeed, it was better than he knew. Although probably it was not what he thought it was, still as a means to a state of faith or a change of mind from the negative to the constructive, it had a very effective mental value.

You see, all of our problems, even though many of them seem to be physical, are actually mental, and the cure is mental even though it may seem to be physical. The physical is a way of reaching the mental and the mental operates through the physical. This is a mental universe and all that we experience is experienced in the final analysis mentally. If I am addressing anyone who has an inferiority complex, or one who is sensitive, or one who has a sense of rejection, or who has a disposition of superiority or arrogance, or one who is jealous or selfish or straitened in finances or unhappy, or who feels just ineffective and fearful, or perhaps one who is prone to frequent anger and resentments, or perhaps one who has insomnia or who is discouraged or weak or feels himself a failure or is just merely anxious— surely I have missed no one now—if I am addressing any one of these, or various combinations of them, then let us set it down quickly that all of these conditions are but symptoms of a dis-eased or disordered mind.

The prefix *dis-* means "not." When we find this prefix *dis-* in the word *disease* it refers to a mind not at ease or not ordered, one which is out of adjustment with the great truth of life, and therefore that mind is in conflict and that conflict is transmitted to the workings of the mind or the functionings of the body or the process of one's affairs. Beneath the surface level of the mind there is the soul, and souls can be in conflict. There is what is called a sore soul. A soul can be as sore as a body. A person's soul can be bruised, wounded and suffering. And whose hasn't been at some time in his life? Who hasn't had his feelings hurt? Who hasn't been sensitive to the harshness of the world? Suppose the wound or bruise has come about because life has dealt the person a hard blow. Instead of reacting in strength the person may have retreated in fear, nursed his hurt and thereby the sore has never got well. So the owner fears the future and desires to escape from the problems of life.

The remedy is to heal the hurt soul. One who has been hurt must necessarily feel that life has rejected him. He may drop into self-pity and self-rejection. The remedy is to cure this false self-appraisal and to make the individual know that he is forever one with the source that created and projected him into being and that oneness gives him dignity and stature and power, not only to endure but to make progress and finally to triumph. If one thinks from the center of a belief in inferiority instead of thinking from his divine center as a divine, whole, enduring being, then he has his attention at an artificial center, and because it is artificial it cannot be productive and effective. Such a person talks, thinks and reacts from this wrong, artificial center. He is, in fact, disassociated from his true center. He has actually lost contact with his true self and like the prodigal in the Scripture wanders in far countries, eating the husks of life when all the while if he had remembered his true center and returned there, he could live and dwell in plenty.

The law of belief is not simple, intellectual belief. One cannot say to another, "Believe in health and happiness and you will have health and happiness." Everybody believes in it but not everybody arrives at it. Everybody believes that he can who thinks he can, but how to teach ourselves to believe more deeply and more wholesomely—that is the big question. It is a matter of training and schooling the mind in healthy-mindedness. After all, we have all spent long years in training the mind in unhealthy-mindedness or just allowing it to be brought up by its influences and reactions. The law that governs the release of true power in our lives is attention. The first sixteen verses of the third chapter in the Book of Acts tell a remarkable story about a remarkable healing. A lame man was sitting at the temple gate called Beautiful and when Peter and John came to the temple he begged alms of them. Peter fastened his eyes upon him with John and said, "Look on us." The account says that he gave heed unto them. He expected to receive money but while his attention was focused upon Peter and John, he received life and strength into his limbs and he, leaping up, stood and walked, and entered with them into the temple, walking, and leaping, and praising God.

Let me ask you, Are you lame? That is, are you unsteady or weak in your supports and securities? Are you unsteady and halt and hesitant in your progress toward your desired goals and ambitions? Then instead of contemplating your liabilities and the oppositional factors that lie in your path, think often of the divine power that gave you life in the beginning, that has never left you, and is now triumphantly resident in your own being at this moment. This central life of your being authorizes you to win and to make progress, and it knows no obstructions and no limitations to its power. One who describes his miseries will never get out of them, whereas one who becomes increasingly acquainted with the divine power within him and who frequently gives it his attention will find his mind automatically tending in the direction of health and happiness and progress in general. He will not have to force himself to believe. Over the track of his attention will come conviction and faith.

"Look on us," and when you "look on us," your mind will get a picture of what you, too, truly are and as your mind holds this picture of what you truly are, your life will be quickened with its realization. You see, one can be lame in the mind as well as in the feet, and a lame-minded man is one who is hesitant and doubtful and fearful, and therefore cannot walk forward into the sunlight. But if he gets a good appraisal of himself lodged in his mind, he will begin to walk forward in his mind, his ideas will be more enterprising and adventuresome and hopeful and he will not be afraid to take risks and to make plans for the future. As soon as his mind begins to walk forward like this, all of his affairs will begin to move in a more constructive fashion. There is a temple gate called Beautiful in everyone's life. It is close at hand. It is the gateway to their dreams, their hopes, their aspirations, and if they could enter within this gate they would be at peace in the realization of their hopes and dreams. However, many sit all of their lives at the temple gate, begging support from everybody else, thinking that they themselves are lame and unable to move by the motive power which God has put into every human being. So long as they believe that their support is outside of them, they will continue to be lame and continue to sit. Until perhaps, on some fine day, someone or something challenges the hidden and unlived life within them and it comes forth in a leap and with a shout and they no longer know that they are lame, having found their feet or their motive power.

All of our progress waits upon a new state of mind. Anything or anyone that can give us that new state of mind is good. The study of spiritual science provides us with valid reasons for getting and maintaining a new and progressive state of mind. The study focuses the attention upon the truth of being and away from the fogs and illusions of life. That is why we advise not mere blind belief, not mere wishful thinking, but belief which is acquired and learned and practiced and sustained by being based upon the fundamental laws and principles of the mind and the spirit. If these laws and principles are followed and sustained, anyone will come out of vexation and into peace, and that means out of weakness and into strength, and again that means out of inhibition or failure into progress and achievement.

Health Is Happiness

I HAVE TOLD AND RETOLD the story about the amateur golfer and the ants. The ball was lying directly on an ant-hill, and the golfer took his stance, lifted his club and swung, demolishing the ant-hill, sending hundreds of the little creatures to glory and disturbing his ball very little. He resumed his position and swung again, killing some more ants but not hitting the ball. After this sort of thing was repeated for some time, there were only two little ants left. They stood there surveying the damage and the critical situation and one said to the other, "If we want to survive, we'd better get on the ball."

"On the ball" is a common expression. Everyone knows in general what it means: it means to be intelligent, to be alert, to be industrious, to be efficient, in short to be in your right mind and to take the best course of action toward your goal.

What I wish to point out is that "getting on the ball" is an act of mind. "All things be ready," says Shakespeare, "if the mind be so." Therefore, it is most important to get our mind ready and then all external and subsequent action will follow the rule of the law of the mind and be in right order and will be efficient and productive. There are definite rules for ordering the mind, and establishing it in right action. The Bible is full of them. One of the better-known ones is this: ''Where there is no vision, the people perish, but he that keepeth the law, happy is he.'' The first thing this verse tells us is that you have to have a line of vision or you perish. You have to have something to work for, some goal to lead you, some purpose to stir your blood, some mission in life about which you can be enthusiastic.

The second part of this quotation from the book of Proverbs suggests that maintaining such a vision is keeping the law; and he who keeps the law, happy is he. The Bible is a book of spiritual law and this little passage is a commentary upon it. The spiritual law is the law of happiness. Some people don't realize that. They suppose that God sends suffering and misery in order to try and to test their souls. But God's law is a law of happiness, and if you keep it, you avoid suffering to a very large extent.

Misery and suffering have only one purpose, to make you search for that law, the keeping of which will remove all misery and suffering. God does not want you to suffer. God wants you to know the law and to be happy. And it is inner unhappiness which is the great curse of the human race. It is my own observation after many years of counseling with sick and troubled people of all kinds, that every kind of sickness originates in some kind of unhappiness. The anxious heart is, after all, only a mental and emotional state, but if it is prolonged it may develop into the real thing called heart trouble. The same thing is true of the lungs, of the bones, of the muscles, the arteries, the skin, and the organs.

Anxiety is unhappiness. Its continued presence in the mind can and does produce pain and degeneracy in the organs of the body. The body is but the register of our emotions, and our emotions are generated by our thoughts. If our thoughts are fearful, anxious, concerned, envious or otherwise dark and gloomy, the emotional stream that flows from these will carry sickness in its current. All forms of anxiety whether about health or about future security or about death or the simple worry about the welfare of others—all are due to ignorance or forgetfulness of the spiritual law and failure to practice this law in one's thinking and feeling.

There is absolutely no reason for continued anxiety about anything or about anyone. The study of the Scriptures and the true science of the soul will reveal this to anyone and enable him to overcome his anxiety.

But before I explain this more fully, I want to say that if you are not yet convinced that health is happiness and that anxiety is sickness, there are many scientific experiments to represent it graphically for your mind. For example, there is the famous experiment that was carried on at Cornell by two scientists, Little and Hart. They tied a light wire around a sheep's leg and then proceeded to send small electric shocks into the leg. This made the sheep's leg twitch, otherwise the sheep was perfectly normal. He went on eating while twitching his leg in response to the electric shocks, but then the scientists produced a real psychosomatic illness, by introducing regularity and apprehension into the shocks. This they did by ringing a bell ten seconds before the shock. This was done repeatedly and monotonously, until finally the sheep ceased eating. It did not associate with other sheep, it ceased to live normally, it developed a real anxiety neurosis. Each time it heard the bell ring, it expected an electric shock. It expected some hurt, an irritation. Now that is what anxiety is: the fearful expectation of harm or hurt.

Notice if you will the mental and spiritual overtones of such a condition. Our text says that where there is no vision, the people perish, and we have explained it to say that where the mind visions a constructive goal and confidently directs its attention toward that goal, that mind is generally happy, alert, efficient and successful. Now the sheep's goal in our story is eating. And he is doing it very well until the scientists send little shocks into his leg. But even these do not matter too much nor keep him from his proper goal. In any average sheep's life as in the average human life, there are many little shocks which come to us every day, but we can live above them. They don't keep us from moving steadily toward our goal or from being well-mannered and cheerful in our daily tasks.

But when the scientists rang the bell and made a mental connection between the sound and the feeling in the sheep's leg, the sheep's mind was withdrawn from its normal attention and vision, was held up and suspended, so to speak. Its mind's attention was directed toward apprehension and anxiety and fear of some outside force doing something to its leg. It could no longer keep its attention upon its eating. It was expecting trouble and difficulty, perhaps doom.

It is the same with people. To be a happy person you have to look ahead, you have to keep your vision upon prospects and goals which hold out good for you, upon good things coming and upon progress being made. This keeps your emotional stream flowing out and forward like a healthy stream from the mountain. "He that keepeth the law, happy is he"; and if he is happy, his tissues will testify to that fact. The law is the way of your mind, and the way of your mind becomes the way of your flesh and the way of your works, the way of all of your life.

Whatever is the basic belief of your mind, whatever holds your attention, your approval, that is the law of your mind, that is the governing influence, the ruling emphasis. We accept one power and one power only. We believe that that power is the Spirit but that it works through our thought. Thought is the one immaterial or spiritual agency we know upon the face of the earth; there is no other. Therefore thought is the agency of God Almighty. And it is for this reason that the great God in the heavens speaks in the Scriptures and says, "I wound, I heal, I kill, I make alive, I the Lord God do all of these things." In other words, negative thought in man kills and wounds whereas positive thought in man heals and makes alive.

Now the anxiety mind believes in powers outside of the human mind. The anxiety mind believes that things are happening to you, not that you are "happening" them, so to speak. This becomes the law of the negative or the anxiety mind. Because of its negative beliefs, it is prevented from visioning happy goals and outcomes and experiences. Because it is always suspended in its vision, its attention is directed to what it fears rather than what it hopes for. In its apprehension it is expecting some blow to fall from the outside, dealt to it by some external power. That was the case with the sheep. Anxiety believes, you see, that you are subject to some mysterious external control. Something is working upon you like a hex or a jinx. You can neither see it nor understand it because it never shows itself.

"Oh, that my adversary had written a book," exclaims the bedeviled and suffering Job in the Bible. For if the enemy had written a book, you could read it and know your enemy's mind and therefore be somewhat prepared for his attack. But this debilitating belief in jinxes and trends and even diseases is due to man's ignorance of his own power. When you do not know your own soul's power to keep you safe and on the right path, you feel inadequate. This inadequacy has to be explained and so you explain it by postulating in your imagination something outside yourself. Now that is excusable in a sheep, but not in a man. A sheep can be controlled by a man. But a man cannot be controlled by another as long as he has normal freedom in society to think his own thoughts. In this blessed society of ours, you have the freedom to think our own thoughts and no one forces you to think his. Then for your own happiness think constructive thoughts. They will lead you, guide you and keep you grazing happily in the pastures of the good life.

It is a law of the mind that what you think most often about, what you secretly love most, what you desire or whatever your attention cleaves to most often, becomes the governing tendency in your life. Moreover, it becomes compulsive and forceful, veritably forcing you into an experience consistent with the imagery of the mind. That is why it is called a law. The constructive vision of the mind is the "good law," and he that keepeth the good law, happy is he. If just 50 percent of the mental attention which people now give to the things they dislike were to be given to the things they would like, what a change great numbers of folk would witness in their lives!

In school one day the principal gave each student three buttons and instructed the students in this way: "One button," he said, "represents life, the second one means liberty and the third stands for the pursuit of happiness." The next day he asked one little fellow to produce his three buttons and tell what each meant. The boy hesitated and stuttered: "Please, sir, here's life and here's liberty, but mama sewed the pursuit of happiness on my pants."

In a figurative way that's what happens to a great many of us. We have life and we have liberty but what do we do with the pursuit of happiness? It gets diverted. Instead of diligently pursuing the upward vision, we allow the mind to be taken over by mass opinion, by convention and by habit until all self-motivation is dead and we are the victim of our surroundings. Then to explain our predicament, we point to things outside the self.

But I repeat, you are not a sheep. Nobody can fasten a wire to your leg to hurt you. There is no power outside of you. Admit none and fear none. Don't hold to hurt in your mind, but hold to happiness and enlargement. Thereby you will be keeping the law of the mind in its highest sense. "He that keepeth the law, happy is he."

Adam, Where
Art Thou?

ONE OF THE CHIEF characteristics of childhood is its
eagerness for information. The recurring theme of childhood is,
Tell us a story. How soon the world complies! Into the eager
open ears of childhood the world mind pours stories of things
to fear. The child soon learns that fire burns, that water drowns,
that certain substances poison, that men cheat, rob and kill, that
parents can be lost, and love denied. In the beginning the child
is not self-conscious; he is innocent of evil, God is present
within him, health is present and Divine Order prevails. But
soon the world mind moves in as we have said, and the child
mind becomes aware that ever so many things of a harmful nature can happen in this world, and then its trust is weakened and
anxiety is increased.

Growing up, which ideally is an unfolding of the patterns of
maturity, is all too often a multiplication of the patterns of anxiety. As the mind of the child becomes more and more taken over
by the mind of the world, he becomes not the child of God but
the child of the world. So often, as we grow older in years, we

become, in varying degrees, wise in the ways of the world. We know our way around in our jobs and in our social circles, but we sometimes have a feeling of being lost and alone. Our spirits are lost. One who becomes spiritually lost must suffer pangs something like those of the child who is lost, only more so. The former things and associations don't satisfy. Old enthusiasms wane and unaccountable feelings of aloneness and impending harm arise. All of this might be tolerable, were it not for another thing. There is something inside of the lost person that torments him by calling his name: "Adam, where art thou?" Whenever any of us is lost in depression or fear or anxiety, he is hiding beneath and within himself and in the shadows of his own fear, and God keeps calling to him. In fact, the reason we are so depressed is that something keeps calling us to come higher and to come out. This something seems to imply that all is not right, that we are beneath ourselves. All of us have been lost in this way at some time to some extent, and all of us have heard the voice calling. Surely we have known, in retrospect at least, that this was no ordinary event.

The solution to the problem of being lost would be easy if only the voice that calls were a human voice. We could answer it and the owner of the voice would come and find us. If someone in the next room calls to us, "Adam, where art thou?" we could answer and say, "I am here in the next room." However, the voice that calls to Adam in the garden is not a human voice, but the voice of Life, and it is so hard to answer. For when it asks, "Adam, where art thou?" we cannot answer for we do not know. Adam does not know where he is. He is lost. The senses can answer a human query and say, "I am here in the next room," but in the case of being psychologically or spiritually lost, one cannot answer because one can be in the lap of luxury, or in his own home with loved ones all about him, with food and warmth and money in the bank, and yet be lost and all alone.

And Something at such times knows that we are lost, and it is that Something that keeps calling to us.

Whether one is lost spiritually or physically and actually, the principle in finding one's way home is the same. Something that has meaning and significance to us calls to us and attracts us. When we make contact with that meaning, we are home again. Some years ago, Professor Maurice Ewing of Columbia University was the head of an oceanography expedition. They were on board a ship, battling high winds and heavy seas two hundred miles north of Bermuda. Suddenly four men were swept overboard. One of these men was the leader, Dr. Ewing. His life was almost snuffed out in those heavy seas, but he was finally rescued. Later that year, Dr. Ewing wrote a remarkable letter to his children about his experience in those seas. In part he said, "I guess you would think that a person would be pretty much alone out there at a time like that. I wasn't alone a bit. It seemed to me that all the good people I love and who love me were there and were encouraging me. Then they all went away and just you children were there. It seemed as though I needed to come and do something for my children. It seemed that all of you—Bill and Jerry and Hopie and Petie and Maggie—were about to drown and I had to come and save you. Then only Maggie was there. I couldn't see Maggie but I could hear her. She was calling to me just the way she calls downstairs when I come home at night—'Daddy, Daddy, my Daddy, come! Daddy, come!' "

Dr. Ewing told his children in that letter that he wanted them always to remember that it was their love which had saved him. He said, "Maggie's love was stronger than those terrible waves."

The Divine Wisdom is ingenious. It knows that when we would not save ourselves for our own sake, we would often save ourselves for the sake of others. It has often been observed that when one is in some abnormal state of mind due to stress or emergency, or the delirium of sickness, the mind projects its own need on to someone else, and then, being concerned about that someone else, it pulls itself out of its own jeopardy. The lost mind must focus. It cannot deal with vastness. No actual voice of little Maggie called to Professor Ewing. What called to him was something real and meaningful in him, and it kept calling him in the midst of the ocean's vastness. Home for him was in his love of his children. God was there in that love and it called to him who was lost in the midst of the sea, and he clung to that and was united with it in spirit and finally in fact. God is always present everywhere and in every situation, good and bad. Actually, God in the form of some meaning, some significance, some Truth, is in every situation, and succor and recovery consist in the mind and the soul making contact with that meaningful Something and hanging on to it until there is union and restoration.

There are thousands of lost souls hiding in the shadows today; some are just wandering aimlessly. Some are feverishly straining after superficial goals. The more they strive for purpose and meaning, the more they sink into meaninglessness and despair. They are lost largely because they are afraid of the Voice that calls. In the Bible story Adam was touchy when this Voice called. He felt guilty; he wanted to hide from the Voice. This is exactly the wrong thing to do and the Voice knows it, and this is why it keeps calling. Don't ever run from events and don't ever try to ignore the facts. Face them and respond to them. In the fact, however cruel it is, is God. Salvation is in the midst of the torment. In the ocean was Maggie's voice calling to her father. The Voice seems to be outside of us only because we are temporarily out of contact with it. But that Voice is the saving element within our situation.

No situation is ever all bad. There is no situation, however bad, but has the element of release and renewal and restoration in it. It is this element that calls to us. It says, "Come out. Stretch forth thy hand. Pick up the serpent by its tail." Forever and again it keeps calling, "Adam, where art thou?" until Adam in us answers. When the mind discovers that no situation is all bad, that there are elements of good and bad in every situation, and "those that be for us are greater than those that be against us," then it begins to emerge from the shadows; and when this thinking comes, we are no longer lost. We have found the constructive element in our situation, the God in the picture, the Christ, the Adam. Now Adam knows where he is. He is here in Eden where God placed him in the beginning. This world, this life is Eden, even though for so long our eyes have been hidden from the elements which make it so.

In any kind of extremity or trouble do not flee and do not hide, but rather be still and listen to the Voice that calls. And when it says, "Adam, where art thou?" be not afraid to answer, "I am here, Lord, in the Paradise where you placed me, and as you made me. I am in Eden, and every precious stone is my covering."

Decreeing Your Good

AN ANCIENT ADVISER makes the bold and encouraging announcement that "thou shalt decree a thing and it shall be established unto thee." Can such a thing be true? Does man's mind have the power of choice and execution? Can a man will where he is going and what he will experience? Is there a power in the human mind to determine the course of events? That seems to be what the old writer is saying, doesn't it? He says, "Thou shalt decree a thing and it shall be established unto thee."

As a matter of fact, each one of us is daily decreeing the events and the experiences of the future by the set and tone of his mind. Emerson says, "The soul contains the event that shall befall it." A man stood on a street corner one time and watched a careless and reckless driver careening down the street. The man observed, "There goes an accident trying to find some place to happen." Observe a nervous, tremulous person trying to accomplish something. You can predict with great accuracy that before too long he will make a mistake or spoil something or break something or hurt himself or hurt someone else. What Dickens called the "dark, dank, damp souls" rarely find happiness even in the most convenient circumstances, because they spread gloom all around them. They are always decreeing more of what they are. So are the happy, constructive people. They likewise decree more of what they are.

Now, someone may say, and quite reasonably, That's all very well, but you don't know what I have had to go through; I have had more than my share of illness, misfortune and losses and mistreatment. And we must answer sympathetically and say, Yes, it is unfortunate and too bad that you have had so much trouble; but if you keep dwelling on the trouble that you have had, you will decree more of it. Such is the character and the force and the power of the mind. You have to make a change somewhere in your thinking in order to decree new conditions in your experience. If you always take your thought from what has happened to you and around you, you will tend always to repeat the experience. At some point you must rouse yourself and be inspired to think something wholly contrary to your experience and then the mind will decree a new set of conditions for you. Many years ago our American poet Ella Wheeler Wilcox wrote, "One ship sails East, another sails West,/By the selfsame wind that blows./'Tis the set of the sail and not the gale/That determines the way she goes." The winds may be contrary but a sailing ship can always get to where she wants to go. She may not be able to travel a straight-line course to her destination, but she can, by tacking, travel a zigzag line to where she wants to go. The determination of her progress is not wholly in the wind but in herself. And that is the way it is with you and me. Conditions are rarely completely favorable but by a mental and emotional adaptation and adjustment within ourselves, we determine our progress in spite of the conditions.

An eminently successful man once confided the secret of his success. He said, "You won't believe it, but it's true. When I was a young man I read a book which was proscribed by my church. I found in it the idea which has been the basis for my whole success in life. The idea was this. If you decide what you want, always keep it in mind and think hard about getting it and you will eventually get it. Twenty years ago I decided to be an investment counselor. I was selling copper scrap at the time and there didn't seem to be any way for me to move from one occupation to the other. But following the idea in the forbidden book, I thought constantly of my objective, and now I am an investment counselor and very successful at it.'' The formula may seem too pat and simple to some people and therefore they won't be impressed; and because they won't be impressed, it will not work for them. The factor in this man's account that is worth noting is that people will often follow a piece of advice or a course of action, if it is forbidden them. The proscription of the book made it particularly impressive to the reader. The central idea in his little formula is rather well known. It can be found in many books. But probably this man would not have been impressed with it had he read it in an approved book. Likewise, he might not have been impressed had he read in the book of Isaiah the description of how a good thought works to bring forth a good result: ''For as the rain cometh down, and the snow from heaven, and returneth not thither, but watereth the earth, and maketh it bring forth and bud, that it may give seed to the sower, and bread to the eater: so shall my word be that goeth forth out of my mouth: it shall not return unto me void, but it shall accomplish that which I please, and it shall prosper in the thing whereto I sent it.''

Isaiah is describing a science of thought. He is emphasizing the demonstrable truth that every idea tends by its very nature to express itself or embody itself in form and function. The power and the force are in the idea itself. You and I do not decree or will anything to come to pass by any particular power of our own; our power is essentially the power of choice by which we choose to think certain ideas and then those ideas by their own native force and with their own mechanics establish their own expression through us. And the key to the whole thing is in the impression it makes upon us; and Isaiah states it in a way calculated to impress. He states the law of thought as a law of nature and compares it to the cycles of seed time and harvest. As the rain and the snow come down from heaven and return not thither but water the earth so that it brings forth next year's harvest, so is a man's thought-content. It is not an idle, purposeless thing. It is meaningful and significant. Things are happening in you and through you because of it.

Your thoughts have consequences. If you want to know where you are going and whither you are tending, look inside and find out the state of your mind and the quality of your thought. This is always the prophet of things to come. The purposeful mind which thinks a little every day of the general direction in which it wishes to go will arrive in good time. But the wavering mind which allows its thoughts to be generated only by what it sees and hears will make progress, if at all, very slowly. Sometimes it is difficult to know what one thinks and therefore whither one is tending or what one is decreeing for oneself. Certain thoughts may become so habitual that they go underground or become unconscious. Yet they go on exerting their influence. A man says he wants to make more money. But he spends money foolishly and seems not to know how to use it constructively. This might indicate that he secretly hates money and resents the fact that he has too little. These two contrary attitudes within him prevent him from making progress. They tend to cancel out each other. Or he is like the man in a rocking chair—going through a lot of movement but not getting anywhere.

A girl may say she wants to get married—that that is a major goal in her life—but she complains that she cannot find the right man. There is something wrong with every prospective suitor she meets. Then we find that secretly she despises men. Again the two contrary ideas cancel out each other or at least cause a great deal of friction and the girl is not decreeing anything good and constructive for her future. I meet many people who tell me that they pray diligently and regularly for certain desirable ends but they get no results. This can only be because they have an unconscious wish or thought tendency in another direction. There is no class of people that Jesus was harder on than the ones he called the hypocrites. And the true definition of a hypocrite is the one who has two opinions about everything. Hypocrisy begins in the thought world, in your mental conduct. If you want to be well-off yet inwardly you feel poor, then this is hypocrisy. It gives rise to the kind of person who announces beautiful ideals, who prays eloquently, who is all for the good and the noble and the true in word and attitude but in his secret heart of hearts he is negative and unbelieving and distrustful. This is the real hypocrite of all times and he is found in many of us—indeed at some time, in all of us. And that is why Jesus took so much pains to point him out and to hold him up as a bad example, as an example of the wrong way to think and to live. He called them in his day whited sepulchers, beautiful on the outside but full of rotting things on the inside. If you put on all the airs of respectability and confidence and good cheer and on the inside feel fear and doubt—you are a hypocrite.

But school your consciousness in the conviction that every thought decrees its own embodiment, not because it is your thought or my thought or anybody else's thought but because it is *thought*. Then think in terms of high-minded choices and know that by the power of a cosmic and universal law you are being led inevitably in the paths of peace and in the ways of pleasantness.

The Master Thought

ONE OF THE GREAT certainties of life is that there is no certainty—at least in conditions and circumstances. Conditions are always changing and there is nothing you or I can do about that. But there is always something you and I can do about our attitude toward these constant changes and that means more than it seems to at first hearing. For our attitude is a handle by which we govern every circumstance and condition that appears in our personal world. No one needs to be like a rudderless ship, storm-tossed and tempest-driven. Our attitudes are the immaterial stuff out of which we can build stability and equanimity and even directive impulses for our life course. There are what I like to call master thoughts which when brought to mind assume an executive control in the mind. A master thought is like a good sheepdog who rounds up all of the strays and wanders and brings together all of the nervous and scared ones into a calm center.

There are many good ways of illustrating what a master thought does before we explain what it is but here is a good one out of the past. One time Dr. Johnson and his biographer, Boswell, were crossing a stormy inland water in a small boat.

The wind was fierce and the waves were enormous. Each wave that broke over the bow of that little boat threatened to swamp it. Boswell was scared—visibly so. Dr. Johnson, on the other hand, displayed all of his well-known philosophical calm and sat quietly in the stern of the little boat. An old Scottish sailor noticed Boswell's growing agitation and handed him a rope. In an authoritative voice, the old sailor told Boswell to hang on firmly to the rope and "be ready when I tell you to pull hard." Boswell got absorbed in this task and forgot a large part of his fear. After landing, he reflected upon all of this for he discovered that the rope was attached to nothing. Holding it could do no earthly good. Slowly, he began to comprehend what the old Scot had done with him and to him—not only out of concern for Boswell himself but because one fearful person in any company is a danger to all of the rest. That old sailor had given Boswell a master thought. He had involved him in something constructive. A nervous and agitated mind is running off in all directions. When the master thought is introduced, the mind is focused and concentrated and becomes immediately effective.

The particular master thought that I have in mind is like that rope. It is something to hang onto; it is something to do when you are agitated, fearful, threatened or disturbed. Unlike Boswell's rope, however, it is attached to something; when you pull it, it does something. We call it a master thought because it masters all of the sundry thoughts and moods and impulses and tendencies which try to claim our attention, upset us, or lord it over us. How compulsive are worries, fears and anxieties and angers and in a generally nervous person how unstable and how fleeting are the thoughts of peace and poise and tranquility! I recall the little boy who was thrashing around in his bed and his parents told him to go to sleep. He said, "I can't go to sleep because I am thinking." "Well, stop your thinking," said one of his parents. Whereupon the little fellow asked plaintively, "How can I stop the think that I am thinking when I am thinking it?'' Of course, his parents were amused with this and could only chuckle to themselves, for they knew the pickle the little fellow was in.

Now, the answer to that little boy's question is in the one word *substitution*. Nearly everyone knows how impossible it is to fight a domineering emotion. Or a habit, which is an emotion gone to seed or one that has been repeated so often that it is now automatic. You cannot by thinking change this emotional dominance. But you can substitute. When the agitating emotion is pestering you, you can consciously and deliberately choose to think about something constructive or you can consciously involve yourself in some activity and some attitude which will beguile the mind from the troublesome emotion. I remember a man who a few years ago was practicing this law of substitution. He conceived of his head as a block of wood—which is not a new idea. But in his case he conceived of his head as made up of small cubes—these were his thoughts. When he wished to introduce a new and constructive thought he conceived of himself as pushing a cube in one side of his head which thereupon caused a cube on the other side of his head to fall out. Somewhat fanciful, of course, and perhaps corny and square; but at least it illustrates the law of substitution. Don't fight that bad thought; simply introduce the constructive one. Get involved in what is right and good and don't worry about what is bad. It will fall away. It will disappear and vaporize itself like fog before the morning sun.

A woman who was dominated by worries and anxieties explained her condition in this way: ''I can't stop myself thinking. The thoughts rush up at me and choke me. I am at their mercy.'' That is the way it seems to all of us when we are in the welter of negative, worrisome thought and feeling. We seem to be at the mercy of these things and are unable to exert any control over them. But that is the great lie. The truth is that each of us, because of what he is and who he is, has a built-in control which he must learn to use. Learning this is what we mean by healthy-mindedness. The undisciplined emotions are like stampeding cattle or marauding animals. They destroy our peace, they undermine our health and they spoil our fortunes. And that is why the undisciplined emotions have been likened to the wild animals which maraud, rend, and tear and kill. But when emotional order is attained, then "the wolf shall dwell with the lamb, the leopard lie down with the kid, the calf and young lion and fatling together; the lion shall eat straw like the ox and they shall not hurt nor destroy in all my holy mountain. For the earth shall be full of knowledge of the Lord as the waters cover the sea." So sang the ancient prophet, and he spoke for all time. The language and the imagery are biblical but the principles are ageless, eternal as the rocks and as modern as today's sunrise.

This healthy-mindedness and this peace of mind come about through the action of the master thought. And what is that master thought in terms of the perennial philosophy and the enduring peace of all the ages? It is called the knowlege of the Lord and that is an old, old name for the executive force of all life and living. The term *Lord* is a holdover from the days of kingdoms and feudal governments. It refers to the chief, the ruler, king, czar, kaiser, khan, mikado, caliph, shah, raja, etc. There are not many of these left today. When we speak of Lord or God or a supreme power, many people think of a person, a large individual; but Jesus has defined God as spirit, and spirit is that stage of life just before mind or thought which in turn is just before embodiment or form or function. Now, since spirit is God or first cause and only cause, then things, people and conditions are not primary and effective causes. They are only suggestive and secondary causes.

A listener in a distant town writes and asks me this question: "How can I overcome feeling angry and resentful as a first reaction to my mother-in-law's unfriendly and hostile actions? I have to live with her." I would suggest that you turn the master thought upon this problem and remind yourself that it is only your body that for the time being has to live with your mother-in-law. Your mind and spirit need not, even though, as you say, your first reaction is to let your mind and spirit be drawn into the condition of your body and its circumstances. But your thought and your spirit are free and they can go to other contemplations. They can think the great truths, such as God is the only Power, and they that be for us are greater than they that be against us, and "the prince of this world cometh unto me and findeth nothing in me." By contemplating such truths you get a leverage over your mother-in-law in your mind and in your spirit. You can do this too by remembering that your mother-in-law is not God; that is, she is not the cause or the creator of your life or your circumstances. Don't give your power away to her. For you, the only creative cause is your mind and spirit. By thinking this, get your mother-in-law out of your hair and create the picture of yourself as living peaceably with her and eventually in your own home. That is the master thought. Follow the logic of that and you will come to rest in the green pastures and beside the still waters of good fortune.

Demonstrate
Your Prophet

WHAT HAS YOUR RELIGION done for you? Has it helped you to solve your problems? What difference has it made in your life, in your home, in your affairs? Has it given you courage? Understanding? Has it enabled you to get along better with others? Has it made you a better workman? Has it made you sleep well? Given you a good digestion? Put you on friendly terms with the universe? And above all has it brought you peace of mind?

If it hasn't wrought some of these wonders in you, and especially the last, it is not religion. Religion is not a creed. Religion is a scientific process of constructive living. It is a method of self-expression. It really doesn't make much difference what your creed is. You may believe in Christ or Muhammad. But you must demonstrate your prophet. If you can't demonstrate your prophet it means you have no prophet. All you have is a statement of doctrine. Action is what counts. Results are the measure of your faith.

"I don't care much for a man's religion whose dog and cat are not the better for it."
—Lincoln

Employ God

I WANT TO TALK with you about employing God in your life. If, literally, you have been having trouble in finding the right person to do the right job in your business, if you have not been able to find the expert advice and information you need in planning a policy and program or in finding the direction of either your business or your personal life, if in matters of health and happiness you have not found the help you need, in fact, if you have any kind of problem at all, then my admonition, to employ God, is for you. For God is the best trouble-shooter, the best consultant and the best advisor on all matters pertaining to human life.

He speaks to Isaiah, the prophet, in these encouraging and meaningful words: "Ask me of things to come concerning my sons, and concerning the work of my hands command ye me."

Now, some people will find it difficult to accept the idea that they can ask God to serve them let alone command Him. Yet these words from our Bible are unmistakably clear and distinct. Furthermore, they are based upon a scientifically demonstrable law of the mind and its action. Therefore, we need not believe them merely because they are written in our Bible. They are true

89

no matter who said them and they would be true no matter where they were written. To make the fullest use of this truth, however, you must understand the way in which it is true. If God asks you to command Him or to make use of His hands, His power and skill and strength, you may feel hesitant. You may say it is presumptuous of me even to think to try to command God, the King of the universe. You might feel that it were highly egotistical of you and even irreverent for you to attempt to use God or to employ Him in your daily pursuits and material needs. This would not be too surprising, because it is the common attitude of a great many people. They think of God as somewhere in the skies, remote and generally unavailable for prosaic details, to be prayed to only in great extremity when human intelligence and strength fail. Many people put God on a shelf to be taken down only when emergency demands.

Dr. Phineas Quimby, a famous mental healer and psychoanalyst of the last century, used to say that too many folk sent for him and the undertaker at the same time. Too many moderns call upon God or the spiritual truth in the same way. They have various reasons for doing so. God is so great and wonderful that He cannot be concerned with my little problems, they think. Or the spiritual truth is so vague and unreal that it is not to be considered practical in everyday affairs. For variable reasons we keep it apart and remote from daily action and on the shelf.

This always reminds me of friends I have who, when they receive a gift of leather or cloth or some other perishable material, proceed to store it away in closet or trunk with the thought, "Oh, this is much too nice to use every day." Whereupon the gift molders away under cover, the years roll on in drab succession and the gift is never allowed the opportunity of sharing its beauty or utility in the common experiences of the day.

Now, this is part of the great gift of God to human beings:

"Ask me of things to come . . . and concerning the work of my hands command ye me." The Superior Wisdom and Power is giving itself to you daily, but if you do not receive, do not recognize and make use of the gift, it is all the same as if the gift were not given. We said that God was the best trouble-shooter, the best consultant and advisor, for God is the name we give the highest and best of everything. God is the name for the highest and the best of everything that you are, of everything that you need or want. Therefore, God is the best of servants, and it should not seem strange to think that man can employ God in his daily tasks. For we find that among human beings, the most successful men and women are those who, first of all, are the best servants. "Let him who would be great among you, be your servant." These are the words of the Master Teacher, and they announce the law of success for any time, in any place, with any enterprise or occupation.

If you would be a leader, you must first become a servant. The best servants are the best leaders. You are a servant to your job and if you serve it well, it will set you on high in terms of success and achievement and remuneration. Perhaps you have an inspiration or a great idea. If you try to outline the path of the idea and to boss it around, you will fail. If you follow the gleam and let it lead you, you will find the pot of gold at the end of the rainbow. Every quickening inspiration is a bridge and a communication between heaven and earth, a bridge by means of which the gods descend and man ascends.

Let no self-willed mind propose to go by any other route than that which is provided him in the inspiration itself. Perhaps it comes to you in the middle of the night. Then you must awake and write it down, lest you lose the inspiration and force of future acts. A person starts to write a novel. His imagination creates some characters and puts them in a situation. Presently the novel takes over the man and writes itself through the person who now becomes the servant of his inspiration.

The Highest Wisdom of God has anticipated this principle in human affairs and has made Himself or Itself the first great Servant that man might imitate Him and rise to success and happiness. God first serves man that man may next serve God. This is the way to the top in any kind of work. "Who has more obedience than I," says Emerson, "masters me." And the scientist takes for his main rule the following: "Nature obeys us in proportion that we first obey nature."

Here is how the principle works: All individual minds are part of a Greater Mind. When you use your mind, you invoke the action of the Greater Mind. All love is part of a Greater Love and when you love, you tune in to the greatness of Universal Love. All power is part of a Greater Power and when you experience legitimate power, you call an unlimited power to your aid. All peace is part of a Greater Peace and when you are still and at peace in and with yourself, you are in league with the angels who know no strife.

Notice that when you employ God you engage His nature, you think His qualities and attributes in your own mind. However well or poorly you do it, thinking these qualities in your mind induces their larger dimensions. For God is spiritual and therefore immaterial. The only immaterial thing we know is the stuff of mind or consciousness. Therefore when we deal with thoughts and feelings, we are dealing with the spiritual realm. There is only one being. It is a unity. This is mathematical necessity. Since it is unity, you are part of it, for you are mind and consciousness. The inside of you is made up of thought and feeling. Your thoughts and feelings are, indeed, a limited degree of the Whole but they are a part of the Whole and when you emphasize them in your thinking, they expand and enlarge and conduct you into the infinite that is the other side of your finite self. You awaken the harmonic elements of your own thoughts and tune in to the larger music of the universe.

If you are not accustomed to thinking along these lines, you may find this a little vague and unappealing. It may not yet satisfy what you think is your need. You may feel that you need something more real and tangible. If you are in bad health, for example, you may say, "It is health that I need and not wisdom and power and peace and love." If it is a job or money which you need, you may feel like the fellow who announced that "There's nothing wrong with me that a million dollars could not cure." But what I am saying to you is that wisdom, power, love, peace and the like *are* money. These all add up to what the Bible calls faith. A modern term for it is confidence.

Where in all the world under whatever conditions, at whatever time, was not confidence immediately translatable into money, vigor, and general well-being? You know it does no permanent good to give money to a beggar. It is temporary alleviation only. If you could give him confidence and initiative, however, you would solve his problem permanently, for having these qualities and functions in his mind, he would never be without money which is the product of these.

So, in spite of the fact that you look at your immediate picture and say that you need money or you need health or you need friends or this, that or the other, I will say to you that you need the *realities* of these things. You need confidence in your own soul as the organ of God on earth. You need faith in divine ideas as the regnant agents of the Almighty. You need to employ these ideas in your thinking more and more until they become the directive agents of your will and of your hand. This is making good use of one's time. It is also the means to real maturity.

You need to employ God in your thinking and acting on the same basis that if you went into a new and highly technical business, you would need to employ the best experts you could find. Moreover, suppose that in your business, you discovered that I was the inventor and owner of secret processes and formulae which were outstandingly superior. In order to meet your competition, in order to stay in business, you would find it expedient to come to me and have me license you to use my process. In that case I would be like God in our present discussion. God is the highest principle, the best method, the shortest and most profitable means of getting anything or going anywhere. You must sometime employ Him in order to stay in the business of living.

"Ask me of things to come." He alone—that is, Mind, consciousness, the spiritual realm alone—is arbiter of destiny. "Character is fate," said the ancient Greek. "Our mind is God," said Plato. Whatever our human mind is, it is some part of the whole, and if we use it wisely it will engage the whole at the point of our operations. "And concerning the work of my hands command ye me." In other words, Power and Wisdom are at hand. Love surrounds you. Peace is available. All these are higher dimensions of yourself. Nourish what you know of them until you perceive their sovereign and divine nature. Serve them in your estimation and respect until they turn and serve you.

God in the
Profit Picture

A RECENT NEWSPAPER ARTICLE tells us that many corporations are hiring chaplains. There may be as many as one hundred business chaplains in the United States. The chairman of the board of one large motel chain gives as his reason for this innovation: "to help bring God into the profit picture." He explains further: "I think God belongs in every part of our lives." That this is an innovation and something entirely new to a lot of people may be discerned in the fact that some object to it strenuously. They want to keep God out of the profit picture. They are of that old school which tends to separate God from daily life and tries to pretend that God (or spiritual principles) has no place in earning a living and in increasing one's prosperity. They seem to feel that it profanes spiritual truths to use them for bread-and-butter ends.

But it has never seemed to me that the greatest of spiritual teachers thought this way. When the people were hungry he fed them bread and fish, he healed the blind man and ate and drank with sinners. He met people at all levels and helped them with their personal ambitions and problems. A chaplain in a business house ought to help that business if he is worth his salt. He ought to be able to reduce personal tensions and help to make workers more efficient, and that in turn will help the profit picture; and there should be no hesitancy on the part of any intelligent person to equate spiritual growth with worldly rewards. Jesus taught that if you seek the kingdom of heaven and its righteousness (or right-use-ness) first, then all these worldly things which men struggle for and are anxious about will be added unto you. An old newspaper editor I once knew retired and wrote homely editorials from his home in the hills. One day he wrote: "I think a farmer's religion ought to make his bull calf better or there's something wrong with his religion."

One of the greatest practitioners of this coordination of the spiritual and the material was the man who made the famous Model T car. I don't know what Henry Ford's formal religion was but I do know that in a significant way he put spiritual principles into practice and they made him rich as they will any person who does so. One Sunday in 1914, when the prevailing minimum wage for factory workers in this country was a little over two dollars a day, news came from Detroit that rocked the industry to its heels and created a sensation around the world, for Henry Ford had announced a minimum wage of five dollars a day and cut the working day from nine hours to eight. Now, he did not do this out of a purely sentimental notion that one ought to be good and kind and generous. He did it as a matter of cold, calculating, financial principle. When asked about it, Ford said, "If the floor sweeper's heart is in his job he can save us five dollars a day by picking up small tools instead of sweeping them out." Later, he wrote: "The real progress of our company dates from the time we raised the minimum wage to five dollars, for then we increased the buying power of our people, and they increased the buying power of other people, and so on.

Behind the prosperity of this country is the enlargement of buying power by paying high wages and selling at low prices."
Five years after that Sunday, Mr. Ford increased the minimum to six dollars a day and said, "Paying five dollars for an eight-hour day was one of the finest cost-cutting moves we ever made, and the six-dollar day is cheaper than the five." Of course, doom was prophesied in Detroit. They said that the Ford Company would fall, that Ford employees would be demoralized by this sudden affluence—they wouldn't know how to spend the money. They said that Detroit would be ruined by an exodus of employers, that those who remained and tried to meet the Ford wage scale would go bankrupt, and so on and so on. But it didn't work out that way at all. It worked out the way Henry Ford thought it would for he said that "The right price is not what the traffic will bear, and the right wage is not the lowest sum a man will work for. The right price is the lowest an article can steadily be sold for. The right wage is the highest an employer can steadily pay."

Cite Mr. Ford's faults and many subsequent errors, but credit him with insight here and in the philosophy with which he carried his insight into practice. Garet Garrett, a biographer of Henry Ford, says that Mr. Ford was the supreme practitioner of free enterprise, a credo and a system that grew to full size in the American environment and nowhere else. It was founded on the doctrine that the individual businessman, freely pursuing his own ends in producing things for others, was bound to serve the common good, whether he consciously intended to or not. In other words, if you want to be a success you've got to give service, you've got to serve people's needs, and then they will pay you for it. As an old newspaper editor I once knew said, "We erect bronze statues of those who grind our axes. Our heroes are people who do our chores. We hurrah for them because they served us." And it was Jesus who said that "He that would be greatest among you, let him be your servant." If you serve people's needs, you cannot fail in any of the goods of this world, no matter what your occupation.

I do not mean to excite anyone's cupidity or sense of greed, only to assure him that if he gets on the right track *spiritually*, he cannot fail in any of the modes of life. It was a great aberration in the old religion that taught that spiritual practice was one thing and this carnal world was another. It separated thought from act, God from man and heaven from earth. Material things were somehow bad and ugly and opposed to spiritual things. You weren't supposed to pray, or to use the power of God, for money or success or love or any kind of personal enhancement. Religion had nothing to do with these and was otherwordly—for a world to come. Nowadays, we see that a thing is not bad simply because it's material. It's the way you use it that determines whether it is good or bad. Money in the hands of a good man is good, and money in the hands of a bad man is bad. It is use which determines all things. The material world is a school in which, and through which, we develop our spiritual powers and learn how to use them effectively and constructively. If we are using our spiritual powers correctly, the material world is not an enemy but rather a cooperative and responsive friend. If one is sick and ailing and miserable and unsuccessful, he is not on the spiritual path, because God never projected such a man as the expression of Himself.

Well, to return to Henry Ford as an example of the coordination of spiritual principles with worldly success, he called it the new method and he said that the method must produce profit. Notice the guiding principles in this method: "Never cheapen the product. Never cheapen the wage. Never overcharge the public." "That," said Garet Garrett, "was the secret of the greatest profit-maker of his age and of any age so far." Ford constantly dispraised the profit motive, which he felt business was always favoring over what he called the wage motive. When business thought only of profit for the owners, "instead of providing goods for all, it frequently broke down—so frequently that scientists had invented what they called 'business cycles.' " Either profits would come from doing the job well, he believed, or they would not come at all, and a properly conducted business could not fail to return a profit. He said, "A business absolutely devoted to service will have only one worry about profits: they will be embarrassingly large." Read the biographies of successful people in whatever occupation and you will find something like this in all of them. They were dedicated to something above and beyond themselves; and that something above and beyond themselves helped them to be what they were. "I will love them who love me and I will be with you, if ye be with me."

In the words of my old editor-friend: "If you would have the world's respect, do its chores. He that would be greatest among you, let him be your servant. If you would be a hero or fill a page in history, attend those who have axes to grind. We love those who benefit us—praise the bridge that carries us over—cheer those who whip our enemies. If you would be blessed, learn to give. If you would be loved, do good. It was a barren fig tree that was cursed."

Plenty and to Spare

WHAT WOULD YOU DO if you were hard-pressed finan-
cially and timid and fearful as a result, and suddenly you picked
up a thousand-dollar bill in the street? It would pay some of your
bills, of course, but would it take away your fear and your timid-
ity? Would it give you assurance and confidence? Could it change
your life and set you on the high road to success and accomplishment and happiness for the rest of your days? That is what it did
for one young man and I shall tell you about him presently.

It is commonplace in many quarters nowadays to suggest
that your thinking has a great deal to do with your health and
happiness but we are primarily concerned with methods and
means of practicing this truth. Our emphasis is upon the laws
of the mind and the way of the inner spirit of a man. The richest
man in the world, we believe, is that one whose inner spirit is
at peace and not in conflict with his environment. The poorest
man in the world, we think, is that one whose spirit is in conflict with things and circumstances and people and events.
Grapes don't grow on thorns nor figs on thistles nor do peace and
happiness and wealth come from fighting and struggling against

100

odds, obstacles and restrictions. The poorest person, typically, is the Bowery derelict, and why is he poor? We may answer it generally by saying, he is poor because he has been too concerned with frustration, guilt, sorrow. He has dwelt upon the emptiness of his life and his mind has eaten up his substance.

In the Bible we read, "I wish above all things that thou mayest be in peace and prosper even as thy soul prospereth." But the soul of the Bowery derelict or of any other restricted and poor person is not prospering. His thoughts are full of weakness, struggle, frustration, fear—and it is these that eat him out of house and home and make him a beggar at the doors of providence and plenty. There is no need of it. A man ought not so to afflict his soul that he cannot live in relative peace and therefore in relative plenty. The world is full of plenty but so many of us are beggars at the hands of life. A little change of attitude, a little understanding of how our thoughts and our feelings govern our experience, an increased awareness of our own inner powers—this is all it takes to change the course and stream and direction of our lives away from restriction and limitation into the channels of plenty and richness.

As with all other human problems, the problem of finance and supply and wherewithal is not merely a problem of economics and opportunity. It is a problem of psychology and religion. It is a problem of the inner self; and the right kind of knowledge about one's inner self and the right kind of practice within one's self, which is another way of referring to prayer, will adjust the inner self, and the inner self in turn will compel a change in one's outward affairs and status.

As an illustration of how an inner change effects an outer change in a person's life, I mentioned the story of a thousand-dollar bill. This is one of those fine short stories by Manuel Komroff. It took place in a little town called Fairview, a clean, orderly little place but a town that was fast asleep until the following happened. Henry Armstrong found a thousand-dollar bill. When Henry picked up the bill he was on his way to his office. His step was hesitant for business was slow with his firm, French and Jones, an insurance company, and during the past months several men had been laid off. Henry felt that his own job was none too secure. Henry was like too many others of today and of all times. He was uncertain and his uncertainty was slowly corroding his mind and therefore his life. Uncertainty brings on fear and loss of confidence in yourself and in your relation to others. Komroff says, "It is an acid that eats into the core of man's nature and changes him into something he should not be."

Here's the difference: In spiritual science we teach one to be certain about spiritual truths, and that balances one's uncertainty about material things. Something like that happened to Henry. He was timid, retiring and afraid of his shadow. But now all of a sudden, what a change came over Henry! He had a thousand-dollar bill in his pocket! He straightened up and his stride became aggressive. When he reached his office, he came in as though the place belonged to him. His boss hadn't yet come in so he ordered, "You tell Mr. French I'll be back shortly. I want to talk with him." Then he walked out briskly to the office of the *Fairview Chronicle*, where he wrote out an advertisement saying he had found the bill: "Owner please communicate with Henry Armstrong." The cost of the ad was one dollar and sixty cents but Henry didn't have that much change and he asked for credit. The clerk had to consult the owner and the editor about that.

"He found a thousand-dollar bill! I'll talk to him," said Mr. Young, the editor.

He went out and spoke to Henry and said, "Look here, young fellow; if you'll give us all the facts, we'll write a news item about this and you won't have to advertise at all."

The newspaper people asked Henry a lot of questions—like what he would do with the money if it were not claimed. He said he was going to marry his sweetheart. They had waited a long time, "But now," said Henry, "we can go ahead." "That makes a good story," said the editor. "Were you born in Fairview?" "Yes, but I don't want to spend my life here." "What's wrong with Fairview?" "Well, it's an old man's town. It's run by a council of fogies who think everything they do is just all right. We younger people feel differently. None of us is going to stay here if we can get out and try a more enterprising place."

Well, you can imagine, if you have not read the story, how Henry's comments looked on the front page of the *Fairview Chronicle* when the townsfolk began to read them. The town became aroused and Henry found himself. He told his boss what was wrong with the business and he told the townsfolk what was wrong with the town. Moreover, he told them all what could be done about it. He quit his job with French and Jones but Mr. French did not accept the resignation immediately. Rather, he said, "Henry, if you'll go ahead with the confidence you have displayed this morning, I'll give you a contract for three years with full commission on all business coming to the firm through you, a twenty-five-dollar raise now and another raise each year." Henry accepted. Of course, I can give only some of the highlights of this wonderful story here. You ought to read it for yourself.

But you also ought to know right off how it came out. When Henry and Dolly had made out a list of furnishings to buy for their new house, Henry pulled the bill out of his wallet and said, "Well, I guess we'll have to use our lucky bill. It would have been nice to keep it." Then, for the first time, he looked at the bill closely and found it was counterfeit. After they got over the consternation and the shock, they laughed. Then Dolly said, "I'm glad the bill is a counterfeit. Now nobody will claim it and we can frame it and keep it for luck. What difference does it make whether it is real or not? This bit of paper made you believe in yourself, started you off to a real future. You've had a raise; you've done more business for your firm than anyone ever did in one week; you've had thousands of dollars worth of publicity; you've got a seat on the city council—the youngest member in Fairview's history. Besides, it's waked up the whole town. Don't you see? The bill has accomplished its purpose just as well as if it had been genuine.''

So that's the story of the thousand-dollar bill, by Manuel Komroff. But there are lots of stories like this. They are happening every day to human beings everywhere. Someone right now is discovering the inner secret of the inner push and will to life. Someone else is experimenting with the nuances of his own thoughts and feelings and discovering their vital connection and relation with what goes on in his body and in his business and in his human relations. He is putting together his own science of life and discovering how to live with greater freedom and with greater plenty. Remember this, that the man who discovers this inner strength in himself is not only a better man and a happier man and a wealthier man in his own life but he is a better man in the community, he is kinder, more moral, more upright, more honest and more cooperative with society. In fact, the whole real system of morality and goodness begins right here with making a man right with himself, based upon the natural law which is in us all.

There is nothing that compels you to suffer limitation and restriction and frustration in your life. If you have been too much hypnotized by your defeats and your failures and your shortcomings, rouse yourself a little from the spell each day and make a real concerted effort to see that your soul is not prospering and because your soul is not prospering, your affairs do not prosper. Observe, too, that all outward, sensibile, external things are but symbols of internal and intangible things. There was no actual thousand-dollar bill, but look what magic the thought of it wrought! For every man the secret of plenty and health and happiness is somehow in the discovery of the executive power and influence of his own thought, using the word *thought* here as a very inclusive, all-encompassing term for the inner content and movement of a man's mind or consciousness. "Man is mind and evermore he takes the tool of thought and shaping what he wills brings forth a thousand joys, a thousand ills."

Hitting the Bull's Eye

To hit the bull's eye, you must miss everything else. The Bible teaches that the knowledge of the One and Only Power is the key to success and happiness. It says that to know God as all there is you must not know another. In other words, there should be no division in your thinking and feeling. You cannot go two directions at the same time. To attempt to work with two opposite concepts at the same time is to demonstrate neither. Don't declare that God is all there is and then feel that the times are limiting your supply.

If we're not hitting the bull's eye it is because we are hitting something else. That something else is usually a belief in error—a fear or anxiety about something external. The Truth is that there is nothing but God and His action. Through discipline the human mind is made to know this beyond doubt or denial. When it knows it, it will not hit anything else for there's nothing to hit. It aims and arrives at the bull's eye—God.

The Eleventh Commandment

THE OTHER DAY a group of us were talking and the subject of an Eleventh Commandment came up. One person said, "Ten I know, but what is the eleventh?" Another voice said, "We haven't finished with the ten yet; what in the world do we need with an eleventh?" But, ten there are and an eleventh there is and I invite you to think with me for a few minutes about them, and I hope profitably. And we shall proceed somewhat after the manner of a student with an examination. He can't answer the first ten questions so he proceeds to the eleventh. It may be that in answering the eleventh question even poorly, he may awaken some dormant understanding of the previous ten.

I have discussed the Ten Commandments at some length in my book on that subject,* but what is the eleventh? We find it in the fourth gospel, the thirteenth chapter and the thirty-fourth verse, which reads, "A new commandment I give unto you, That ye love one another; as I have loved you, that ye also love one another." There is really nothing new about it because all religions teach love and good will. All true philosophy enjoins

*Ten Words That Will Change Your Life (DeVorss).

it. Common sense honors it as a worthy goal. Psychology and medicine insist upon it as a necessity for health and happiness. Certainly one can never be inharmonious with others or with his environment and have his tissues and arteries healthy nor his business dealings successful. If you hate, your glands know it and will tell you about it, and if you love or are at least generally harmonious, your glands and organs will not talk back, but rather remain silent and by their silence let you know that all is well. The old physician's aphorism says, "The healthy know not their health." If you are healthy, your nerves do not talk nor your bones cry out nor your stomach sound any alarm.

But the commandment is new for anyone who has not yet found peace in his life. The average person begins his life with resistance and frustrations and angers and as he approaches maturity discovers that it is an absolute necessity to compose himself inwardly and find some working relationship with others and with his environment generally or he cannot go on. I remember hearing a highly placed government official, now retired and world-famous for his good humor and geniality and his rare ability to gain the cooperation of widely differing individual minds, saying that he owed his success to his discovery at about the age of thirty that he was given to despising and belittling other people in his mind and he had to learn to appreciate them for what they were and to get along with them as they were. Former President Eisenhower affirmed in public print that he knew why he got his heart attack. He said that his army temper rebelled and exploded at the red tape and devious ways of bureaucracy and politics in Washighton. He learned how to take that in hand and to compose himself, and his recovery was an inspiration to all.

So the commandment to love is not new in the history of philosophy and religion. It is new only in the individual experience. It is not new from the point of view of a moral edict. It is new only when one begins to practice it. But nobody can practice a commandment handed down from On High. All commandments are made to be broken. Whenever and wherever you make too many rules for people, those rules will be broken inevitably, for without understanding and inward composure a man cannot arbitarily and by self-will obey or keep a rule. It is not in the average man to obey a rule simply because somebody tells him he must. If the rule or the law is not in him as his own understanding and thought, he will be unable to obey it. You notice this happening wherever you see such a common sight as a Wet Paint sign. That sign—Wet Paint!—means Don't Touch! You know what happens. A certain number of people don't believe in the sign or they rebel at being told what not to do, or the very command of what not to do suggests to them to do it. If we say to the child, Don't put beans up your nose, he is intrigued with the desire to try it.

If you analyze the word *commandment* as it is used in the Scriptures you will find that it does not mean merely an edict handed down from some superior authority but rather a new directive from within—a new direction in our thought and our psychology which expresses itself in a new way of acting and living. Jesus never taught commandments and edicts and rules and regulations. He taught self-change and rebirth. If what he taught had ever been truly learned by one-third of the population, there would be no war, no conflict and cruelty, no neglect and inhumanity. For he taught that the way to achieve right action in oneself and in relation to others was to get the thought right first. It is as hopeless to get a right action out of a bad thought as to hatch a chicken out of a bad egg or to produce a plant out of nonviable seeds.

A man cannot decide to do something good merely because he wishes to. He must have the internal emotional force for it or his wish and his will are impotent. Notice how the alcoholic in the days before he acknowledges that he is powerless to control alcohol, often boasts, "I can take it or let it alone." It is a proud boast and it comes from something instinctive within him and it is true ideally but not always functionally. While he boasts that he can take it or let it alone, *it* is taking *him*, and his will is impotent because his psychology is not capable of backing up his wish and his will.

Out of the heart are the issues of life, not out of the head. Each of us is always living under the compulsions of his own habits and conditioned emotions. We do not what we wish, but what we must, as compelled from within. And all change, to be significant, must be inner change concerning what one thinks and what one feels. In learning any skill we have to develop an emotional backing for it or we fail. A man may have all the figures and facts; he may have gathered all of the knowledge concerning his project, but if his psychology is out of tune, he will fail. All true force is truly spiritual. That is why the wisdom of the very first verse of the very first Psalm says, "Blessed is the man who sitteth not in the seat of the scornful." Scorn people in your heart, belittle them in your thought, despise the time in which you live, and no matter how many other strengths and skills you may develop, you will come somewhere, sometime to grief and fail in your most cherished aims.

The late Ely Culbertson, the brilliant bridge expert, and a man who was undoubtedly brilliant in many directions, bragged that the beginner with a brilliant intellect can overcome inexperience simply by thinking his way along. By sheer force of intellect, he said he could break ninety in a golf game for eighteen holes the first time he played. "I am a brilliant mind," he said shyly. He tried it and lost miserably and then blamed bad luck. "My intellect was working but the ground was bad and my clubs were out of line." Whether he said this with tongue in cheek, I don't know; but taking the facts as they are related, we must say that he himself was out of line and that is why he did not succeed. Anybody who plays golf knows if he thinks too much about all the rules and tries too hard to fulfill every requirement, he plays poorly. At some point in every game, and surely most of all in the game of life, one must learn to relax and to let go and to allow a higher power to take over. Study, work, practice and discipline—all of these are necessary in the beginning— but at some point you must learn to do what you have to do with relaxation, and experience that thrill of all true doers and achievers of having something bigger than your intellect invade your brain, take over your hands and dispose of your knowledge and your skill and your talents in its own superior and inimitable way.

When you come down to the pure psychology and metaphysics of this matter, you will feel compelled to see that Jesus was not talking of people alone when he said, "Love ye one another." He was talking about our thoughts and the occupants of our minds. The love of people outwardly is possible only when there is love or harmony among our own private thoughts and attitudes. The heart of a man must ordain peace or his hands cannot achieve it. In the story, the disciples to whom this commandment is given are men of flesh and blood. But, in the inner account which the story illustrates and symbolizes, the disciples are the disciplined qualities of the enlightened mind.

What is our mind but a group of faculties and their functions? They are vision, attention, faith, judgment, imagination, will, enthusiasm, perseverance and so on. What these faculties do in an individual mind determines the functions and the actions of the individual person. If the mind is filled too much with superstition, resentment, fear, prejudice, anger or jealousy, then such a person with such occupants in his mind cannot love, he cannot feel harmony and the commandment to love will either fall upon deaf ears or provoke him to the exact opposite. He cannot love because he projects what he is upon others. And seeing the repugnant reflection of his own disorder in others, he blames and resists them. Of such an internal disharmony are all the wars and cruelties and hurts and sufferings of the racial experience generated. I said that Jesus did not make rules and teach creeds and regulations and commandments as ordinarily understood. Over and over again he emphasized that we have nothing to deal with but our thoughts. That it is here within each one that the gospel must be preached, that the good news must be heralded. When one gets a grip on this, he may reason away his fears and his resentments. And as Jesus cast the moneychangers out of the temple, so the individual may cast the thieves of his life out of his own temple of consciousness; and finding peace and well-being within may confidently ordain it without, in his body, in his human relations and in the works of his hands. The healing of our own minds is our only work. When this is done you also project what is within to that which is without but instead of blame and censure, intolerance and anger, good will and harmony flow like a river. Then health abounds and happiness gathers and Love fulfills the Law.

Be Good to Yourself

SOME YEARS AGO I had a friend whose motto and watch-word was "Be good to yourself." He always closed his letters to me with this expression, and whenever we met and then parted, he always left me with a smile and a wave of his hand—and with this cheery bit of advice, "Now be good to yourself."

My friend was a great teacher and healer of men's minds and bodies. He loved people above and beyond their faults and miseries. He seemed always able to look right through and beyond a person's limitations and faults and see and talk with the true self there. He was a man who was looking back on history when I met him and no doubt it had been many years ago that he had adopted this motto and this greeting, "Be good to yourself," because he had seen how hard on themselves people often are. There is no more mistreated person in the world than the true self of the average person. We all know people whose hearts throb in sympathy with the whole world but they neglect self and are not good to themselves in their thoughts.

It is this true self and not the historical Jesus of whom the prophet Isaiah speaks in these words: "He is despised and rejected of men; a man of sorrows and acquainted with grief."

Open your Bible sometime to the fifty-third chapter of Isaiah and read this whole chapter with this idea in mind and you will receive great illumination and instruction and come away with wisdom and strength. The divine Saviour of man is not in history but in man and he is forever crucified, not on a cross of wood but upon our fears and our guilts and our inferiorities. God has placed His laws in our inward parts and written them in our hearts. We read that we are made in His image and after His likeness. The divine nature, therefore, is in our human nature. When we reject this, we reject our true self and clothe ourselves in sack cloth and ashes and sit down to weep for our own depravity and sin. So it is this true self in man who is wounded for our transgression, bruised for our iniquities. He is oppressed and he is afflicted and brought daily and continually as a lamb to the slaughter.

My friend saw this—how people afflict themselves and condemn themselves and that was why he tried to get everyone he knew to be good to himself, not merely to indulge his appetites and his pleasures but to be truly good to the divine being that lives and breathes in every one. The great scourge of the world is fear and inferiority. No one ever hurts another who has properly approved himself. It is anger in the heart, anger against our own self that makes us strike a blow at another or say an unkind word or spread some evil tale, or subtly, smiling and serpent-like utter some seemingly harmless phrase with a sting or a barb hidden in it. There could be no war were men not at war with themselves. All those who wage war and all those who cry out against war will have to understand this first.

There is one basic enemy for all of us as there is one common friend and that is the Divine Being that lives and moves in each and every one of us. How can that Divine Being be an enemy? In the same way that fire or electricity or atomic energy or any natural force can be an enemy when we incorrectly relate ourselves to it. The Psalmist describes this warfare that goes on inside of a person when he says in the forty-first Psalm, "Yea, mine own familiar friend, in whom I trusted, which did eat of my bread, hath lifted up his heel against me." This is a way of pointing out that the mind of a person ought to be a friend to all the rest of that person. The mind's concepts and estimates ought to be wholesome and generous and constructive, for if they are not, they grieve the spirit within and the true self suffers as a consequence. Therefore, we are counseled not to grieve the holy spirit of God within us.

All experience is reactive to our thoughts. It we think evil, we shall experience evil and if we think good, we shall experience good. This is the mental law that governs all experience and all human activity. The mind is the leader of the procession. If its estimates and convictions are low and mean, then the reactions of the body, with its organs and functions, are miserable and limited. The spirit within, which should find free and unfrustrated outlet through our mind's thoughts and concepts, is cramped and confined in narrow channels until this inside spirit weeps because we will not give it outlet through hope and faith and generally constructive thought. Think of the great scourge of inferiority that afflicts mankind universally. Egotism and aggressiveness are problems in the world, to be sure, but they are not nearly such a problem as inferiority. Thousands afflict themselves and accuse themselves needlessly. They have too small an estimate of their powers and capacities. They measure themselves unequally against other people and events and prospects and goals.

Then why should men think ill of themselves when the Great Universal Directive whispers and shouts to every man, "Gird up now thy loins like a man for I will demand of thee and answer thou me." You may recall that in the Bible Job, that most miserable of all men and therefore the symbol of all misery and limitation, says to the Lord God, "Behold, I am vile. What shall I answer thee?" It is in the words just quoted that the Lord responds to him and says, "Gird up thy loins now like a man. I will demand of thee and declare thou unto me. . . ." He continues, "Deck thyself now with majesty and excellency and array thyself with glory and beauty. Cast abroad the rage of thy wrath and behold everyone that is proud and abase him. Look on every one that is proud and bring him low and tread down the wicked in their place. Hide them in the dust together and bind their faces in secret. Then will I also confess unto thee that thine own right hand can save thee." What a tremendous announcement! What illumination! What a wisdom! *Your own right hand can save you.* In other words, the power of the Almighty—that is, enough of it to live your life and to do your deeds and to fulfill your ideals—is locked up inside of you.

The realization of this power is to be found, he says, by decking yourself in majesty and arraying yourself with glory and with beauty. It is your low, mean, limited concepts which hold the majesty and the strength of your being away from you. By enlarging your estimates and convictions about yourself and about life in general, you will enlarge the channels through which this majesty and this excellency can and will express through you. Your health will spring forth speedily. Your prosperity will be increased. Your love and appreciation and fellowship with other people will flourish and the opulence and abundance of your life will rise to overflowing in blessing for yourself and for others.

Why can't you think more highly of yourself and be good to yourself as my old friend suggested? Your mistakes and shortcomings have not corrupted the real you. It is still there. It is still awaiting your belief and understanding. It is your friend and it can help you. Moreover, it wants to help you but it is powerless to enter the activities of your life without the belief and the acceptance of your mind. If your mind has been turned, as is the habit with people in the world, too much to the external picture of things and the history of men's sufferings so that the suggestion of fear and harm and suffering is borne too much in upon the mind, then of course you will have to stop frequently and remember that externals are not causes and that nothing can happen to you except by the movement or by the sufferance of your own mental processes. Listen to the way the Scripture says it: "God hath not given us the spirit of fear," and "Give not over thy soul to sorrow; and afflict not thyself in thine own counsel. Gladness of heart is the life of a man; and the joyfulness of a man is length of days. Love thine own soul and comfort thy heart and remove sorrow far from thee for sorrow hath destroyed many and there is no profit therein. Envy and wrath shorten a man's days and care bringeth old age before the time. A cheerful and a good heart will have a care of his meat and diet." Or, as my old friend, who still waves to me in memory, says, "Be good to yourself."

Tell No Man

TELL NO MAN your secret wish or dream or the subject of your prayer. It is your Father's business and no one else's. Prayer, to be effective, must be secret. A secret must not be told to anyone. If you talk too much about what you are going to do, you will never do it. Withhold your speech until the action can speak for itself and you. Many dissipate the force of good resolutions and prayers by talking too much about them.

An old story illustrates what happens in such an instance. The Emperor Frederick the Great asked at a dinner gathering of his advisors, why, when taxes were so high, not enough money reached the desired sources. An old general fished a large piece of ice from a punch bowl and passed it to his neighbor and asked that it be passed around until it reached the Emperor. By the time it reached Frederick it was about the size of a walnut. The general sat down. The lesson was obvious.

Like Frederick's lost tax money, your lost dreams may have been handled by too many people. Mind your own business. Go, and tell no man.

The One in Ten

NEW TESTAMENT READERS are familiar with the story of the ten lepers who were healed and the one who returned to give thanks. The account relates that when Jesus entered a certain village, ten lepers met him, stood afar off and lifted up their voices and said, "Jesus Master, have mercy upon us." He said, "Go show yourselves to the priests." As they went, they were cleansed and one of them, when he saw he was healed, turned back and with loud voice glorified God and fell down on his face at His feet, giving Him thanks. And Jesus answering said, "Were there not ten cleansed? But where are the nine? There are not found that returned to give glory to God, save this stranger."

There is not only inspiration but profitable instruction in a Bible story like this. The first thing we must ask is, Who is this stranger? Is it strange that only one out of ten should return to give thanks for his healing? No, that is not strange. In fact, it is quite common—common then as it is common now. Nine out of ten people do not perceive the significance of an event nor are they able to feel grateful and thankful. Some simply do not see. Some are too bound up in their own emotions. Some are slothful, some are rebellious, some are just plain indifferent. The percentage, therefore, is probably just about right. About one out of any ten will perceive the significance of true values in his life, will count them first and be grateful for them and go on to health and happiness. The others, even though they are made well by the laws of the Spirit, will not perceive those laws and will go on taking their health for granted and be none the wiser. So we may say the man that can perceive and be thankful for the spiritual principle in his life is to a great extent a stranger in the world. He is not the common, ordinary, average man.

Next I think we can ask the question, Is this stranger perhaps in ourselves? It could be. None of us has ever been perceptive and thankful enough for the true values which sustain our lives here on earth. We take our youthful vigor for granted until we begin to lose it. We take a good night's sleep for granted until we have difficulty sleeping. Then it takes a long time for the mind to rediscover what the soul always knew—that He giveth His beloved sleep. When tensions and troublesome emotions steal our peace of mind and cause our blood to boil, raise our blood pressure, disturb our pulse rate or cause splitting headaches—these are some of the great host of psychosomatic ills which are nowadays attributed directly to poorly trained emotional life—it is then that we may begin to discover that some element has been omitted in our living, that some part of us is missing. We may suspect that we are guilty of some sin, that we do not love God enough or that we have not learned to pray correctly or prayed enough or some such thing.

But basically, the problem is in the fact that we are not well enough acquainted with our spiritual self. By spiritual self, I mean our higher mental self. You see, there is another person behind our personality in every one of us. There is a greater self behind our little self of which our little self is only a partial showing. This Greater Self is quite adequate for all the problems in the world. He comes equipped to solve every problem and to handle every incident and situation. But we do not know this at first and so this Higher Self who could think correctly and establish right action and manifest wholesomeness and goodness and who could establish for each of us our validity and prowess as a spiritual being, completely triumphant in his environment, is not recognized, not perceived, not understood.

This is the stranger in ourselves, for the discovery by an individual of this spiritual self which heals his diseases and lifts him out of misery into happiness is not a common occurrence among men. It is unusual. It does not happen to all men at the same time. It happens here and there among certain individuals. For example, the person who has had a strong feeling of inferiority since childhood and all of his life has been running before the circumstances and situations and demands of life and whose tension and stresses have been building up within, giving both mind and body a terrific beating for years, suddenly ''comes to,'' so to speak, and discovers that he need not run, that there is nothing that is chasing him. He begins to discover his higher elements and his larger dimensions. He begins to discover that mind is a creative force and that as a man thinketh in his heart, so is he, that this is the only creative principle and the only creative power. Therefore, it is God among men or on earth, and since it is the Only Power, there are no other powers opposed to it. Therefore, the devil is a liar from the beginning. He is not a self-existent entity but a concept of the mind.

Such a man begins to have a rebirth in himself and discovers the stranger in the world, the spiritual self who is in the world but is not perceived by the world. As John tells us: ''He was in the world but the world knew Him not.'' For the Christ man is not merely an isolated instance in history but is a universal spirit and a universal intelligence, always tending toward birth and rebirth in individuals everywhere. But it is not common or usual for people to throw off their stresses and their tensions and their hates and their resentments, their illusions of dark powers, of terrors by night and pestilences by noonday. It is common and usual for most men to struggle with these and to wallow in the turmoil. Therefore, when a person does throw them off and discovers his higher potentials, he rises out of his indifference, his sloth and his ignorance and discovers the stranger within himself.

When we are in disease and tension and stress, the true man is a stranger to us; he is unknown. The man of composure and of peace and of faith is not known to the person of turmoil and disturbance. That is the person we are looking for in ourselves. I do not have to tell you that he lives in you. You feel it deeply within your heart. As Phillips Brooks once said, ''We feel the thing that we want to be beating beneath the thing that we are.'' This is a spiritual truth, dimly and instinctively perceived by every individual who stops to think about himself. It is not true because I said it or because Phillips Brooks said it. It is true because it is in the heart of every individual and no sophistry or argument of any kind can dispute what the heart tells us is true. So we are all looking for that man, that perfect man. When the disciples of John come to Jesus, they say, ''Art thou He that should come or look we for another?'' This stranger is the God-man, the true self, for he is so strange in this world of pseudo-selves and partial selves, of false selves. This stranger is involved in all of our false and pseudo-selves but he is not seen or recognized commonly.

In medicine there is what is called the disease of schizophrenia which means a split personality, the Dr. Jekyll and Mr. Hyde type of personality. Metaphysics and religion recognize the same thing. We also speak of multiple personalities. We have all known individuals who, under different circumstances, different times and places, exhibit different personalities. The deranged man in the Scriptures, when asked what his name is, replies, ''My name is Legion for we are many.'' Most of us, I think, can understand what multiple personalities are like because we find the seeds of them in ourselves, every one of us. The Greeks gave us our word *personality*, and it means a mask. The personality of every one of us is a mask which hides the deeper levels of our being. For example, every one of us is trying to put his best foot forward all of the time. We are trying to make an impression. I do not mean that we are always dishonest in this or that we are imposters. For example, when a person has a headache and feels as though he should go home and go to bed but he still smiles and carries on and is affable with people—that is his personality. He is wearing a mask for he is masking his true feelings. Every one of us feels the seeds of many different types of personalities within himself.

To illustrate it very, very simply, when we are depressed we are one kind of person; when we are happy and elated we are another kind of person. When we are resistant, we are still another kind of person. When we are free and flexible we are still another type of personality and so on and so forth. We all have the many within us. Most of us have some degree of integration and union of the various personalities, otherwise we should have no individuality at all. But oftentimes when a person becomes the victim of many tensions and stresses and fits and starts and seems to have no control over himself, he is like the ten lepers who met Jesus. The personality is all split up into many drives, impulses and reactions. There is no singleness to the personality, no union, no sense of self and therefore they are called lepers in the Bible because a leper is one whose flesh is disintegrating, except that in this higher level of interpretation, the leper represents *a mind* which is disintegrating, divided and being split up. It is without blood or livingness.

The number of ways in which each of us can be in error is legion, but there is one way to be right, and that way is to believe in yourself because you believe in God—to believe in your spiritual powers, inherited direct from the Godhead, to believe that God made you upright and it is not your business to seek out many inventions of evil and destruction. When you do begin to believe in this way, you will meet the stranger in yourself because the ten, the divisions, will be integrated, the many will become one; and that is why the story tells us that only one returned. Because only one ought to return, only one *can* return. When the divided, split-up personality is healed, the many are united in the one. When we are brave enough to let go of our false personalities, to give up our opinionated judgments and preconceived opinions and foolish roles, then we shall find that we have lost nothing but the zero. The Real Self, the Eternal One, the one that God made to dwell above sorrow and misery is still there as he was always there, and it is he who is said to return to give thanks to the Truth that saved him.

This or That

IT'S GOTTA BE this or that. So goes a popular song. So goes life. Man's mind is working with one or the other of two ideas all the time: Good or bad. Success or failure. Confidence or fear. Peace or trouble.

The difference in the amounts of time you spend thinking about these two general subjects determines your achievements and your happiness. In any given situation, so long as you live, you have only these two to think about. Nothing else. Your wisdom or your ignorance will determine the way the balance falls.

The person who knows God scientifically—not just through hearsay—will think most often of God or good. Another, being ignorant of God, is forced to dwell in doubt and fear.

You cannot go in two directions at the same time either physically or mentally. What seems most reasonable to you, that you will follow—God if it be God and error if it be error. Therefore study to know that those who take the citadel of heaven are "not of double heart" (1 Chr. 12:55).

The Power That Makes Things Go

A CERTAIN VICE PRESIDENT of these United States said that he did not begin to succeed until he was past thirty-five. About that time in his life he ceased quarreling with other people in his mind. I met another man like that just the other day. In fact, I've known him for years. He has always made a fair living, but never enough. There was always a struggle. The other day when I met him he told me this arresting news. He told me that his business volume was three times what it was last year and this in spite of the general slowdown in other businesses like it. He attributed this welcome change in his financial status to a significant change in himself: he had given up fighting people in his mind. He had relaxed and come to peace. He said, "You've told me about this for years but I only now have understood."

He had learned an important lesson, namely, that we have never anything to deal with but our own thoughts. If and when we live harmoniously with our own thoughts, we shall live harmoniously with all other people and things and animals and conditions. This is a law. We have no enemies but our thought of enemies and we have no opposition but our thought of opposition. Understanding this, we know another thing: that there is no cause for bad feeling. When we understand that there is no cause for bad feeling, we can dissipate it and get rid of it.

These two men I have mentioned were both well prepared for life. They had good education and training and experience. They had everything going for them but one thing going against them and it was their tendency to quarrel with others in their minds. At least one of these men had also great religious faith but his faith was generally impotent because he lacked good feeling. It is a Bible statement of the great Mental Law that "Faith works by love." You can have all the faith in the world but if you do not hold it in the presence of good feeling for others, it is impotent. Faith works only in the presence of good feeling. It is like a chemical catalyst in whose presence other chemicals go to work, and when the catalyst is absent the other chemicals remain inert.

In one of the most profound and at the same time most poetical pieces of writing in literature, the thirteenth chapter of First Corinthians, Paul held forth on this Mental Law of Faith working by love. There he observed that if you had faith enough to move mountains but did not have love, you were nothing. You may be very knowledgeable and skilled also but if you do not use these in the presence of love or good feeling, you will not be successful. You may have all the virtues and a great personality and overflowing generosity but if you lack good feeling within, you will be obstructed and restricted all along your way. I am putting it in prosaic and everyday language because the old words of the Bible often lose meaning by their very familiarity. But if you get a glimpse of the principle we are discussing here, then go to the thirteenth chapter of First Corinthians and read it often. Listen to the opening words: "Though I speak with the tongues of men and of angels and have not charity I am become as sounding brass or a tinkling cymbal." The whole piece is a great commentary upon the Mental Law that "Faith works by love." Another statement of that Law is: "Love is the fulfilling of the Law." Of course, love has so many connotations and meanings to so many different people. But let's simplify it by just calling it good feeling.

Recall again the old verse: "A man may smile and bid you hail, yet wish you with the devil; but when a good dog wags his tail, you know he's on the level." Because the average dog just overflows with good feeling. It is so natural and whole-souled to him; and fulfilling the Law means that all the virtues, all the skills, all the acquisitions of learning and ability work best and most efficiently and productively only in the presence of good feeling. In society, the law is plural. There are so many laws that not even a houseful of lawyers can remember them all. These laws generally set forth the rules for right conduct among people. Nearly all of them are prohibitions against bad action toward others. But one who has a good feeling within himself has fulfilled all the laws that were ever written or ever will be written because he will not even be tempted to offend others in word or act.

It is said that one of the biggest lobbies in Washington is the education lobby. It is composed of people wanting to spend more and more on education. Now no one can put down education, but why not educate in the things that alone can make all other knowledge and skill work? If you have all the knowledge in the world and have been to all the best schools but are still little and peevish within yourself, your education counts for nothing. You will be a failure. All the while that you are applying your great skill and knowledge, you will be losing force inside, which force is simple good feeling. It is a pity that in many of our scientific researches we have to rediscover rules which have been available to us for three and four thousand years.

I have written on the work of a Baltimore pediatrician. He has been studying children who eat and drink all the time but don't grow. These kids even scavenge garbage cans and drink from mud puddles. Doctors have described them as having the "Garbage Can Syndrome" and also the "Mud Puddle Syndrome." Scientific tests show that they lack growth hormones. But the main difference between them and true dwarfs is that these children will grow if taken from home and placed in a different environment. Most of the studies show that they are totally unloved by their parents. A typical case is that of the mother who does not want the child even though she may not admit it; another case is the alcoholic father who is away a lot. All these researches point strongly to the fact that what these children need is love. Then they will grow. But even an abundance of physical food of which they can never seem to get enough will not enable them to grow without this mental and spiritual food which we are here calling simple good feeling.

Research on dogs has shown something similar. Normally an electric shock will increase a dog's heart rate and blood pressure. But the simple act of petting the animal while it is being shocked, holds down the heart rate by half. Doctor Gampt, who ran these researches at Johns Hopkins, adds this additional and arresting observation: "No more than the presence of a person in the experimental room softens the shock's impact."

There is great inspiration in this research but also, as I indicated, a great pity. The inspiration comes from the fact that here we have fresh evidences of an ancient rule and law, namely, that God is Love. Simply put, that means that the "making" power is love. The creative power is love. What makes things go is love or good feeling. You can have all the knowledge in the world but if inwardly and secretly you despise or are hypercritical or if you belittle others or sneer or scorn, then your knowledge will not be fruitful because you are deficient in love or good feeling. You can have great powers of personality and great religious faith but if you are too easily outraged by what others say or do or if you are too easily incensed or you resent too long, then you are losing force within and the great power which you have acquired will dissipate itself in inaction and failure. History is replete with examples of unlimited power without love or power without harmony—they are people who seem born to set the world on fire and to change the course of history, but move like comets across the sky and then fall miserably and go out like a light. There are also countless examples of men and women who come into this world with small endowment, have an adequate education, who never got the big breaks but who nevertheless seem magically to succeed in spite of all that was against them. Look at them and in most of them you will discern their secret—they had good feeling and in the presence of that good feeling their meagre endowments flourished and what little they had worked wonders because it was used in the presence of the great catalyst.

Heredity Is No Alibi

IF I WERE to announce a title for what I want to say in this article, it would be "Heredity Is No Alibi." It is a truism that we cannot singlehandedly reform the world. We can only reform ourselves. I prefer the word *transformation* to *reformation*, and the Bible points out that we are transformed by the renewing of our mind. To learn how to do this takes away burdens imposed by heredity. All metaphysical study and psychological practice show this to be true. Our minds are merely collections of records. They are filing cabinets of all of our impressions and sensations which we have accumulated during our lifetime. The mind is nothing of itself; it is a medium between the unformed world of spirit and the formed world of matter.

Spirit is the substance and the essence of life. Matter is the formulation and the expression of the spiritual essence. Mind is the medium which modulates or transforms spirit into matter. That is why holding an idea or an image in the mind allows the spiritual essences to take form and function in the material world. Since ideas and impressions and sensations form what we call our mind, to renew these ideas and impressions is to transform our mind and our world.

131

In order to renew the ideas of the mind, we have to get some fresh slants and viewpoints on life in general. This in turn requires that we be flexible enough to give up some old ideas and viewpoints in order to make room for the new. It is obvious that what we are aware of constitutes all of our experience in this world. Without awareness there would be no sights, no sounds, no warmth, no cold, no light, no dark, no sweet, no sour, nothing but void and blankness. Awareness or consciousness, then, is cause and awareness is faith that makes material things and sensations reality. Our state of mind is our faith, and all things are according to our faith.

Since all of this is true and much of it is self-evident, it makes little difference who your ancestors or what your heredity. But what a great deal of difference people tend to make of these! Folks are so eager to excuse their failures and their unhappiness by reciting such tales as this: "I come from a broken home." Without intending to be flippant, we can say, "So what!" The butterfly comes from a broken home and his broken home promotes his glory as a butterfly. The ugly duckling in the fairy tale comes from a broken home, but as Albert Edward Wiggam observed, "It makes no difference if you were born in a duck pond so long as you come of a swan's egg."

Others will complain, "My father was an alcoholic and my mother was highly neurotic. What chance did I have?" And we must answer, "The chance of a lifetime." For in company with all other human beings, we have two inheritances, one from men and one from God. It is important to know the difference so that we will remember the swan's egg rather than the duck pond.

Let us consider first the inheritance from men. You have had about sixteen thousand ancestors since the pilgrims first landed on these shores in 1620, provided there has been no duplication in the twigs and branches of your family tree. These ancestors gave you the color of your hair and your eyes and these you cannot change. They handed you your mental and emotional susceptibility towards such things as laziness, moodiness, nervousness, hypersensitivity, fearfulness, stubbornness and many other qualities and characteristics. These you can change, for they are not native and absolute, but rather acquired and learned.

Heredity offered you nervousness perhaps, as a first choice. This is what we mean by susceptibility. But you did not have to accept nervousness and if you have accepted it, you need not retain it. This is what we mean by free will. No man has free will as regards a learned, acquired and conditioned characteristic or quality. But every man has free will as regards the possibility of changing that characteristic and acquiring another. Habit rules, but thinking makes habit.

Our ancestors do, indeed, make us according to their image and likeness in so many thousands of ways. But in all the ways that matter, there is nothing absolute or unchangeable. There is an appeal from every condition and every kind of bondage and every promise for release from the bondage. We cannot ignore the fact that our parents and their parents before them have written their mental and emotional characteristics in our genes and in our cells.

Another way of saying it is to observe the old philosopher's maxim, "The dead rule." The dead, indeed, do rule. Their thoughts and emotions and tendencies and drives and temperaments and dispositions are alive in the thousands and millions of their descendants. Ambition and greed and inhumanity to man all walk abroad today in the present generation as inherited characteristics from generations long gone to dust. Many a child is spoiled simply because you cannot spank grandma and grandpa. We are the victims of our heredity, but I repeat that all the characteristics which we have inherited from our human parents are learned, acquired and copied and are not inherent constituents of our nature.

Let us consider the inheritance that we have from God. Our parents did not give us life. The life that came to us was filtered through our parents and qualified as it passed. But the life itself is the Spirit which comes directly from the Universal Life and Spirit of all things. From our heavenly Father we received the principles of our nature, the principles of the cell structure, of the ovum and the sperm and of bodily formation and its maintenance. From our heavenly Father we received the capacity to think, to reason and, therefore, to change or to renew the mind, and by that means, to change the whole of our lives. From the Universal Life we received all mental and emotional possibilities in infinite variety and in unending duration.

How we exercise or make use of these possibilities is the subject of our individual choice and will. For example, we receive from the Universal Life the capacity to love, yet there is a wide range of choice in this inherent capacity. It may be expressed either as hate or lust or as great good will and infinite compassion. The habit of use is acquired by man but the capacity is inherent and unchangeable. All men at last will come to the correct and happy use of their powers inherited from God but until then, they will be under the force and sway and bondage of acquired habits and copied patterns of thought and feeling and action.

So our heavenly Father is the only true father there is, for Spirit is the only cause, the only presence and the only power. All material forms and expressions are simply the manifestations of that one presence and power called Spirit. Conditions do not make other conditions, but what conditions do is to inspire thoughts suggestively in minds; and minds, by their own creative power, proceed to create duplicates of the conditions which inspired these thoughts. So does history repeat itself through the years because men blindly follow the thoughts of the past and make no creative change by transforming their minds.

All of the good attitudes and emotions and qualities are inherent in each one of us. They are there mostly as dormant and unrealized capacities; all together they are called the Son of God for they are the offspring and generation of the Supreme

Power, the spiritual mind. To become aware that these are in us, to appreciate and understand them is to hear the Voice say, "Thou art my beloved son. This day have I begotten thee."

Self-realization and spiritual maturity come to a person when he makes contact with his own inner spirit and he talks with it and it talks with him and he finds an anchorage in something deeper and greater than the outer facts of his life. In all of us there is a layer of habit and acquired characteristics lying between the inherent spirit and our understanding. It is this that stands between God and us.

All of this means to us that when we look to our heavenly Father and our true inheritance and realize our inherent capacities as sons of God, then we have power over our own life by means of this spiritual inheritance, and it does not matter then what our human inheritance may be.

When you tend to speak of something you "inherited" from your parents, cross out the word "inherited" and insert "copied." This will express the situation more truly. What has been learned, acquired and copied is not permanent but constantly subject to change and rectification. Prayer and meditation, and especially scientific prayer, are the means of rectification. Remember that your spiritual nature is from God. It is the Son of God, and unto the Son He saith, "Thy throne is forever and ever: a sceptre of righteousness is the sceptre of thy kingdom."

Let us have the boldness to ascend the throne and wield the sceptre. Many a peasant's son has been taken from the field and into the court where he learned the wisdom and the art of kingship. It could never have been so were kingship not already within him, not as the son of the peasant but as the Son of God.

You will get results from your prayers if you will every day endeavor to lift your sceptre and brandish it boldly over the situations and conditions which would tempt you into fearfulness or anxiety or despair. All things make way for the strong Son of Light.

The Secret of
Personal Power

LET US BEGIN by suggesting an old spiritual exercise which is practiced and has been practiced for centuries in the East, which will illustrate our subject—the secret of personal power. This, in turn, will give birth to another kind of exercise which we can all practice with great profit.

Think of your breakfast toast or any kind of bread you may have had for breakfast. Now begin to trace it back to its origin. Where did you get that bread? If you had breakfast at home, you or someone connected with the home bought the bread, carried it (or it was delivered) from a grocery store or a delicatessen. And where did the store get the bread? A truck from the bakery delivered it to the grocer. Keep going back as though you were to take a moving picture of the evolution of bread from grain and then run it backward. In the bakery you see the bread coming out of the shipping room. Behind that was the wrapping room where it was wrapped. Before that the baking ovens where it was baked and before that the mixing bowls where it was mixed.

The beginning of bread is further back yet. The essential ingredient of bread is flour. The flour came to the bakery in bags delivered by a truck. The truck picked up the flour at the railroad freight yards probably. Keep on going back in imagination and follow the freight cars perhaps to the big mills in Minneapolis or somewhere else where it was ground into flour. And then go back beyond the grinding process to the delivery of the wheat to the flour mills. Perhaps it came in great freight cars and we can see it pouring out through spouts into the storage bins of the flour mill. And then let's follow the freight trains taking it out of the great storage elevators in some town or city in Kansas or Nebraska perhaps and see the farmer hauling it to these storage bins in his trucks from the farm. Then look at the harvesting process where the farmer first produced the grain.

Go still further back and see the wheat growing; look at it just coming up out of the ground; look at the planting of it by the farmer. He began with kernels of wheat, bushels of them. Along about here we shall come to the end of our exercise in meditation for we can go no farther back than the germ of the wheat. We have been all through the visible process and now we are back in invisibility. The generating core or center of all this process by which our bread comes to our breakfast table is a little bit of life in a kernel of grain which is entirely invisible. All those kernels of wheat which we feed on today came from one kernel of wheat. Conceivably if one kernel of wheat had been planted in King Tut's time and its offspring replanted repeatedly, we would have enough wheat to feed the whole world many times over. Out of one kernel of wheat we would have an infinite number of bushels of wheat and an infinite number of bags of flour and loaves of bread. Such an exercise in imagination leads the mind back to the realization that all manifested things come from an invisible life. It leads to a sense of this invisible stuff which is the sustenance of all of our living. Any physical thing upon the face of the earth can be traced back to this unanalyzable residuum which is basic energy or pure essence of spirit. And God is Spirit.

When you get there, you are in the presence of God. So I suggest this as a form of mental exercise which will strengthen the mind for its greater works in prayer. It is a way of accomplishing what the book of Job advises, "Acquaint now thyself with him, and be at peace: thereby good shall come unto thee." This exercise also will help in accomplishing that which Jesus describes in these words: "Yet a little while am I with you, and then I go unto him that sent me. Ye shall seek me, and shall not find me: and where I am, thither ye cannot come." The secret place of each person's world is his thought. No one can follow him there unless the two are attuned. The Secret Place of the Most High is spiritually perceptive thought. The secret of personal power is found by going often to this place in consciousness. Let it be noted that by personal power we do not mean power over people. We do not mean influence among people or delegated authority such as a politician or an officeholder may have. Political power is the delegated power of a people. Money is a power of which some people have little or none. These are some of those kingdoms of this world with which the devil tempted Jesus and at one time or another they have tremendous appeal to each of us. Personal power is magnetism. It is soul force. It is discipline of one's own thoughts and feelings and control of one's own consciousness.

When you get into trouble as a human being, rise in thought to God. Acknowledge your oneness with the Infinite and then the Infinite becomes the only actor on the scene and the solver of your problem. Emerson said that "the humblest person when contemplating God becomes God." This is the highest kind of prayer. We wish to acquaint ourselves with the higher power that it may invade our littleness and displace our weakness. We wish to acquaint ourselves with the Infinite to the extent that the Infinite shall become the only actor on our scene and the solver of our problem. There are many degrees of acquaintanceship at the human level. There are nodding acquaintances, the

"Pleased to meet you" sort of thing. There are close friendships and intimate relationships such as that of man and wife, brother and sister, parent and child.

If one has reached only that point at which he thinks of God as a mysterious power, something that cannot be known and is impractical even if it were known, and he shies off from thinking about it and deals only with what he can see, touch, taste and feel, then the inner world of such a person is subject to disorder and confusion, for the spirit has not yet begun to move upon the chaos of the mind.

Perhaps one has gone one step further and realizes that there is some ruling order, some higher power, some ruling life principle, but beyond that he is not willing to venture. Then the unknown to him is vast, authoritarian and cruel, and he often tries to propitiate this power by sacrifice, by penance or rites of worship. But by virtue of his own premise this power is apart and opposed to him, whatever his propitiatory exercises may be.

Let him go further and find power as the very essence of his being. Let him take up some such exercise as we have cited with the bread. Let him find the common denominator of all life.

The central principle which is the root of all things in Life—not life as we know it in fish, fowl, animal or man, but Life which is anterior and interior to these many forms of life, the undifferentiated before it becomes differentiated and the unmanifested before it becomes manifested—is pure spirit. At this point all life is one life, simply because it has not yet been diversified as fish, fowl, plant, animal or man. This is the common denominator of all life, unknowable but not unthinkable. This is the secret place of the Most High, the Father's house to which Jesus said he went and to which each of us is privileged to go when he has the proper basis in thought. Here at this point in thought one loses his identity as man or fish or animal and becomes pure Spirit or God. Now hear again the words of the adviser to the ancient Job: "Acquaint now thyself with him, and be at peace.'' At this point in realization one cannot be troubled, dismayed or disturbed or weak or fearful. Acknowledging his oneness with the Infinite he finds that all qualities which belong to the Infinite belong also to him. Because It is strong, he is strong. Because It is calm, he is calm. All that he ever wishes to become in fact, he now is in essence. This is the Presence, the only presence, for all analysis of matter, mind, emotion, leads us back to this basic energy or essence, and the act of going back in thought and realization to this primal power is the second exercise that I referred to in the beginning.

Having found your way to this secret place and awareness, return often to it. If it thrills you to return you may be sure that you are there. And now take this as the departure point for your new kind of living. When you have gone backward through matter and function and form and identified with the timeless, ageless essence and acknowledged yourself to be that, then begin to return and to think from this point of view forward into matter and time toward the manifestation of the ideals that you would like to express.

Think of the Infinite Power as pure Spirit and of mind as its medium, then hear the ancient word that was born of this high realization: ''Thou shalt decree a thing, and it shall be established unto thee.''

Don't Apologize for Success

NO ONE NEEDS to be told that life is an art. We have all experienced the difficulty of the artist, to make his hands and feet do what his heart and mind see. We are all earth-bound but dream-driven. Artistry is in making the two come together.

But we all need to be reminded of this frequently—that life is an art and that we are all artists and that we must be diligent about the daily business of performing our art. That is why in these pages we turn the lights of our attention and intention upon some phase of the art of living. When Newton was asked how he accomplished so much, he answered, ''By intending my mind.'' The road to the hot place is paved with good intentions, we are told, but so is the road to every other place; for intention practiced long enough leads to action. Therefore let us strengthen our intention again and again until the force generated thereby takes hold of the flesh and makes it walk in the path of our intention. That is the law of life—in the beginning is the word or thought or intention, and the word becomes flesh or form or movement. Practice is the secret—doing the right thing over and over again until the spiritual agencies of life are awakened in your behalf. There is no profit in any philosophy or religion without daily practice. It is so easy to forget to live, to allow the vexations and griefs of outer existence to suggest loss, defeat or suffering to us. Daily attunement of the thought to the laws and principles of religion and philosophy will bring affirmative and life-giving suggestions to the mind. This is practice, and practice is living.

Not long ago it came to my attention that two people I knew were failing in this regard. They had come under the spell of sickness, either their own or that of others, and instead of looking at their difficulties and reacting to them in an exactly opposite manner to the way the difficulties suggested they ought to act, they had been going down with their difficulties. They had been brooding over them and allowing the emotions of distress and depression to overwhelm them. Now this is common and human and ordinary, and we cannot afford to censure or to blame. But we must remind these folks to stir up the gift of God that is in them and resolutely set their minds against the suggestion of their circumstances. When sickness comes or loss accrues, the circumstances suggest that all is gone: give up, retreat, mourn, surrender and let the blow fall. Instead, let hope and faith on the inside also send suggestions to the mind. They say: Do not believe what the facts suggest. The disposing cause in your life is your thought and not your circumstance.

In addition to intending and coercing the mind in positive and affirmative directions, there is a correlative law to be learned well and practiced continually, and that is the Law of Harmony. This means that you must never think for another what you do not wish to have or experience for yourself. For we are all one. When we look at each other we seem to be all separate individuals with spaces between us. That is true physically, but spiritually we are one body. Mentally and psychologically we have community with each other. Each of us emits a kind of mental-emotional atmosphere, and these atmospheres mingle. Take the very word *individual* and note what it means. Superficial thinking suggests that *individual* means "separate and apart," but it means basically "indivisible." Spiritually speaking there is only one individual in this world, manifesting itself in the form of all the billions of human beings plus all the animals and fowls and all other forms of life. These are but variations of the One. This One is indestructible, birthless and deathless, inviolable and beyond all pain and hurt. Whenever you are in trouble think of yourself as this One and immediately you are lifted above your trouble. Continue practicing this thought and the trouble will vanish from your life. Joy will come in its place. Peace will come. Right order will come and all your circumstances will begin to harmonize themselves in a wonderful and magical way. Beware of dwelling in criticism upon another, for this amounts to *self*-criticism and *self*-destruction—because we are all one.

There are people, however, who have not learned this Law of Harmony—or if they have heard of it they do not practice it. Because they do not practice the Law of Harmony their otherwise constructive thought fails. There are people who love great music, for example, who have not found the harmony of their own spirits. There are people who love great art on canvas or in stone who have not yet appreciated the art of harmonizing their spirits with others.

The very first verse of the very first Psalm in our Bible gives direction about this point. "Blessed is the man that walketh not in the council of the ungodly, nor standeth in the way of sinners, nor sitteth in the seat of the scornful." As we have pointed out elsewhere, this verse speaks of three motions or rather three positions of the body and symbolizes, by these, three attitudes of the mind. The verse speaks of walking, standing and sitting. Walking "in the council of the ungodly" means intending the mind in the wrong direction, giving ear to untruths and hearsay, accompanying in thought some living imagery. To stand, means to give full attention and become absorbed in the situation at hand. To sit, means to accept as a mother hen sits on the eggs until they hatch out into chickens. A mind often sits on an idea until it hatches out into form and function or activity. Blessed is the man who sits not in the seat of the scornful, who does not adopt as a settled attitude of his mind the scorn or depreciation of other people or their works. Scorn and snobbery were once the special sin of aristocracy. In history it is exampled best perhaps by the famous remark attributed to the French Queen Marie-Antoinette, who, when informed that the common people had no bread to eat, is said to have exclaimed, "Let them eat cake." But extremes meet, and everything changes to its opposite. Today it is not the aristocrat but the peasant who has been taught to scorn and hate. The wealthy are scorned and ridiculed and blamed and the poor are glorified and set on high. Enterprise which has for its aim any private gain or personal advancement is looked down upon. The tendency in this kind of thinking is to minimize achievement, to ridicule ambition and to neglect enterprise. In some quarters it goes so far as to make people feel that they ought to apologize for their well-being or their wealth or their good fortune. It is frightening to contemplate the ends to which it might go: instead of honoring success we would honor failure; instead of encouraging the dynamic and talented ones among us to thrust forward on new tangents of enterprise and daring and accomplishment, we would train them to go around in circles and remain in the same old place.

Don't ever let yourself feel constrained or obliged to apologize for success. The whole movement of life is from invisible to visible, from thought to thing, from word to flesh, from dream to manifestation, from subjective to objective. The universe is inexhaustible, limitless in its possibilities and potentialities. The very purpose of life is to get richer in all ways and in all dimensions; to develop the art of living. Emerson says "The very strife of trade and ambition is expressed of . . . divinity." Divinity is the spirit-life seeking form and function through the flesh, the hands and the brains of men. We ought to rejoice when we see another succeed. He demonstrates our own unused powers and encourages us by his example. The Law of Life is from thought to thing, and the more things we can bring forth out of our own thought, the more we shall grow and the happier we shall be. Never can we possibly exhaust the infinite riches of the infinite life from which we draw.

Don't let the evil philosophies rob you of your enterprise, your daring, your boldness, your faith, your hope, your vision of bigger and better things. At the same time remember that this attitude must be balanced by a remembrance of the Law of Harmony; keep your thought true and free of scorn, envy, anger, hate and discord. Then your thought manifests in Divine Order, for the Divine Mind has no such moods as these just named. Enterprise of thought and reach of mind and hand, plus remembrance of the Law of Harmony, will take a person as far as his vision can reach—and no one can place any limits to his strength. Each is free and unobstructed and unconfined now as a spiritual being. Let him think this and go forward; let him love what he thinks are his enemies as Christ taught, for in Truth he has no enemies save the thoughts in his own mind. Let him do this as it is taught "that ye may be the children of your father in heaven"—that ye may be the perfect expression of that Life which has generated you. "I came that ye might have life and have it more abundantly." Don't ever fear that abundance. Desire it. Don't apologize for it. Rejoice in it. At the same time grant to every other person in the world, good or bad, his right to the same abundance on the sole condition that he will fit himself to receive it by visioning high and by loving others.

Keep Well

I HAVE A FRIEND who has lived a long and eventful and fruitful life. He passed the proverbial three-score-and-ten mark some fifteen years ago and is still going strong. When friends ask him, as they frequently do, how he maintains his health and vigor, he tells them his general philosophy which is, *Keep* well instead of trying to *get* well. Don't allow yourself to degenerate to the point where you have to struggle to get well again. He goes regularly to his doctor and he goes regularly to church. He observes the basic rules of health and frequently knocks off his busy schedule to go to a spa and rest and rejuvenate. With his physician he follows the ancient Chinese custom. He pays the doctor to keep him well, not to make him well after he is sick. He is a metaphysician in his thinking, and that means that he uses the law of mind in actively and daily envisioning himself as well and foregoing all melancholy and depressive thinking. He doesn't like to associate with people of his own age. "They are too old," he says.

As you can guess, from just this much, the important thing in this man's life is his vision and estimate of himself, his constant communion with health and vigor in his mind. Without this, his doctor could do little for him. So often, when one gets sick, all the physician can do is to administer a pain-killing drug

146

which gives one the illusion of being well and thus gives the mind a breathing space and enables the mental factors to go to work. There is only one real healer and that is mind or consciousness or psychology or the spirit of a person. Many other things like drugs are helpers and aids but they are not the healers. Even a common drug like aspirin does not heal. It simply shuts off or inhibits the feeling of distress and the person feels relieved and the mind says I feel better and his whole psychology and spiritual thrust begins to affirm well-being instead of a fever or pain. This helps to make him better.

Now, the great reason why this works as it does is, in the language of Genesis, that God made man in His image and after His likeness and that is why your personal vision of yourself is effective. God made you by imaging, for it says He made man in His image or by His image or through His image. It does not say that God is in the shape or form of man, and therefore man is made after that image. No, it means that God, who is formless and without body or shape and is therefore Mind, can create in only one way, and that is by imaging, or the projection of ideas. Hence God made man in or by or through His image, and man came to be. Now since God made man by imaging and after His likeness, He gave to man the same prerogative on a smaller scale that God has on a cosmic scale, and that is the power of imaging, or what I like to call *imagineering*. That is why your personal vision is effective in all things concerning you. Indeed it may be called the Presence of God in you.

To repeat, God is not a body or a localized entity but the pervading presence of universal Mind in everything and through everything; and that is why the Bible, and especially the Psalms, bids us praise It. To praise something means to count it first, to rejoice in it, to think frequently of it; and that in turn builds up confidence and facility so that when one images his health and his happiness and general right action in his life, he will not at the same time discount it or disparage it or sabotage it by thinking that it does not work or that it is just idle daydreaming or futile fantasy. On the contrary, he will image with confidence and assurance and know that just as "the thing I feared has come upon me," so will the thing I love come to dwell with me. Be assured that whatever you live with in your secret imagination will come into your experience.

Generally, people little understand this tremendous principle. They get tired or bored of being told by religion to praise a God who allows so much pain, so much injustice and hurt in this world, because they are thinking of that old-fashioned God who is dead—a big man in the skies or some kind of invisible potentate living in invisible splendor and judging men below. But when we think of God more scientifically, we understand that God is Mind both in Its universal aspect and in Its particular and individual aspect, which is man. At either end of the scale, its potency is the same in kind if not in degree. All thought is creative, whether it is good or whether it is bad. Your thought is creative. Be careful what you think about; you will get it. Be careful what you dream of or imagineer in your heart; it will come to live with you. The universal law is automatic and not capricious.

As we think, so we are; and as we feel, so we go. There is a reaction to every thought. Nothing punishes us and nothing rewards us except the reaction of our own thoughts. Nothing outside of us can do us harm nor can it bless us except it come through the medium of our mind. We are already blessed in this arrangement, for it gives us leverage over ourselves and our conditions. The thing is to see it, rejoice in it and go forward bravely, knowing that this is a reciprocal universe which honors our most sustained and constant thought by manifesting it as our experience. Therefore, if you praise this power and think and see yourself as well, you will be well. For you will be guided all along the way as to what to do and what not to do and how to think and feel and act in such a way as to maintain good health and good fortune.

But seeing yourself well is more than just a mentally contrived picture of yourself as well. It must be a fully rounded thrust of the whole nature toward right order in your life. Order, as we have heard, is Heaven's first law. It would be folly to mentally see yourself as well and then quarrel in thought with your environment or with another person. Just as it would be in error to make pictures of yourself as well and happy and then at the same time indulge fears or anxieties or deal in disdain and scorn and criticism and cynicism. These latter attitudes deny the former and cancel them out.

In contrast to the first friend I mentioned whose philosophy is *keep well* instead of always struggling to *get well*, I have another friend, a woman, who makes frequent trips to the hospital in order to *get well*. She has long espoused this philosophy which I preach and teach but at the same time has always been sensitive and critical in her thought—good-naturedly so, but nonetheless sometimes petulant and carping. Avoiding these attitudes is part of the visioning that keeps one well. She has to learn to fill her mind and her heart with peace and harmony; and if conditions irritate her she must learn to turn from conditions and consider the great truth that "Great peace have they who love thy law and nothing shall offend them." If you see the Law and understand it, it will beget great peace in you in spite of the most irritating conditions.

Let go and let God; return to your Father's house, for your Father is always there waiting to nourish you. You have no enemy, no obstruction, no barrier to your progress. Therefore there is nothing to be offended at or by. You can live in a world of sixes and sevens, a world of many injustices and wrongs and still not suffer, because you know the Law, or the Lord, and you praise it or him night and day. As the poet says, "You do not have to fight, you only have to know." Understand the one and only power, love it and praise it. As Mother Teresa, the Catholic saint, says, "Love God and even your enemies will be constrained to bless you."

Don't Be the Victim

IT IS SAID that James Watts discovered the principle of the steam engine by watching a teakettle boiling and the lid bouncing up and down with the escaping steam. And the analogy is often made between this phenomenon and the explosive force of human emotions. A person often has to "blow off steam" or to release tension or work off his aggression and hostility. And this in turn suggests that there is a fire burning in every one of us, an expanding energy trying to get out and to go somewhere. Why does a person "blow his top" if not because some expanding force within him meets with some restrictive or inhibiting conditions or situations? There is something in you and me which wants to go somewhere, and it will go in one way or another in spite of all that you and I can do or say. Whether it goes in divine law and order and creates good for us or whether it explodes violently and wreaks havoc in our own lives and in the lives of others depends upon our understanding of this explosive force within.

The very meaning of our existence from the time that we are born until we die is to desire, to reach, to express and to do and to be and to have. And if this thrust of the deep-lying levels of our life finds happy exits and smooth expressions, we are fulfilled and we are healthy and we are happy. But as all too often happens, when this thrust of the spirit is thwarted, delayed or frustrated by conditions and people, then tension builds up within, the creative forces are congested, the pressure mounts and if our understanding cannot find a safe and orderly way of releasing these tensions and pressures, there is usually an explosion such as a fit of temper or a display of anger or a nervous collapse or something of the kind. And it is in these periods of frustration and congestion that disease develops, because disease in the body is just what the word itself implies it is: dis-ease in the mind and spirit.

Every steam-boiler has an escape valve through which too great a head of steam can be released harmlessly so that the boiler will not explode. Every electrical circuit is protected by a fuse containing a little piece of metal which will melt and break the circuit before the heat in the wire gets so great that it can burn the house down. Every human mind needs its safety devices also to protect itself from explosions which are destructive. "The Lord is a strong tower and the righteous runneth into it and is safe" is one description of such a safety device. For the concept of the spiritual law which governs all things enables one to see that no condition, no situation, no circumstance and no person has in and of itself or himself the power to prevent the true expression of every true desire of a human heart. "God hath not given us the spirit of fear but of power and of love and a sound mind."

Where then does the spirit of fear and frustration and anger come from? From our misunderstanding of events and circumstances and other people. Once understand that the power that gives you the desire, the urge, the dream, the hope, the wish to go forward and to make your life better also gives you the power to fulfill that dream and to express that hope and to achieve that wish in divine law and order, without penalty and without hurt to yourself or another, and you have an insight and a concept which will reduce tension, break down the inhibiting factors and destroy the walls of frustration so that tension and pressure will not build up. The engineer of a steam-boiler can release an excessive head of steam through the escape valve but he seldom makes use of this because if he is a good engineer, he is continually releasing the steam which he manufactures in constructive ways—he is releasing it into radiators to heat homes and offices and he is releasing it into machinery to turn wheels and to do work. The force which would otherwise destroy is made to serve useful purposes and to achieve satisfying ends.

Learning how to do this with our emotional pressures is the need of every person. Rage destroys more people than war because it is allowed to build up internally until it explodes in some negative way. And there is no need for rage to be built up to such proportions. Conditions are not against us and circumstances cannot long thwart the righteous impulses of a healthy mind. People may indeed seem to get in our way here and there, but people cannot thwart the spirit of Life which understands itself, for it is not only power but it is wisdom. It cannot only do, but it knows *how* to do, and it knows how to do it in the *right* way; and if one trusts this simple insight then he can learn to release his inward pressures in constructive ways so as to achieve health and happiness for himself and others.

The Scriptures say that "A man's enemies are they of his own household" and the first household in which you and I live is our own mind or the inner recesses of our own consciousness. The real enemies are here within. They are our doubts, our fears, our rages, our jealousies or perhaps our scorns and hatreds or our erroneous beliefs that conditions and people and institutions stand in the way of our health and happiness. So long as we believe this and accept it, it becomes the ruling factor in our lives and we run when nothing pursues us or we simply sit still and smolder in the fumes and heats of our own making. No one can harm us if we first do not accept harm in our own thought. No one and nothing can thwart us unless and until we believe that that which is outside is greater than that which is inside. This realization then is an escape valve or a fuse by means of which the overload can be reduced. And it is also a means by which our psychic machinery can work constructively and release the pressures of our desires and intentions and wishes in methodical and harmonious ways and in constructive works and achievements.

I said that rage kills more people than war. It also maims more people than war. The other day I read of a young man of seventeen who went into a bar and insisted that since he was so close to legal age he should be served a drink. The bartender refused. The young man went out and pushed his fist through the plate glass window and cut himself so severely that his left hand had to be amputated. Soon after that he was in another fracas in which his rage induced another man to shoot him through the wrist of the right hand. While surgeons were trying to fix him up, he ran out of the hospital and at last account they feared for gangrene in this hand. Rage is such a terrible thing because it builds up the pressure so quickly and that pressure of a creative force, because that is exactly what it is—a creative force going wrong—explodes and tears apart when otherwise it might create and build. And the whole problem in all of this is that so many people do not understand how "fearfully and wonderfully we are made." Those who do understand have learned to give place to wrath, to avenge not themselves, to accept the thrust of these unseen forces in themselves as basically good and to learn to turn the mighty stream of creative force into constructive channels.

This misunderstanding of the spiritual forces inside of us which can create peace and harmony for us but which often, when unwisely managed, create just the opposite, was long ago observed by St. Paul who said, "The good that I would, I do not, but the evil which I would not, that I do." And the late Fritz Kunkel, a wise doctor of the mind, called this famous statement of St. Paul "the beginning of depth psychology." Everyone who has examined himself knows that at times he cannot seem of his own will to do what he knows it is right for him to do and he also sees that that which he would not like to do, he seems forced to do by these unconscious forces which act above and beyond his will. It is a situation of contraries. The conscious mind wants to go in one direction and the subconscious mind wants to go in another direction. This is not because they are basically enemies but because the individual does not understand the forces deep inside of him, which are seeking expression through him. He is incorrectly related to them.

If a person has not accepted the Will of God for himself as health and happiness but rather believes that there are evil forces in the world which can deter, delay or thwart him, then his subconscious energies take this form and pressure him into disagreeable experiences to confirm the premise in his mind. But if on the other hand a person does resolutely accept the promise of God in him as health and happiness and continually expanding good, he then relates himself correctly to the deep-lying forces and they build up pressure which compels him into good just as formerly they might have compelled him into error.

Our inner, subjective power is seeking higher levels of expression all of the time and if we understand it and cooperate with it, it can lead us into meaningful experiences and take us from strength to strength and from joy to joy. Another way of saying this is that the angels inside of you want out. And I don't care who you are or what you are, there are angels in your nature, for God is your Father and it cannot then be that you are anything but nobly sired and nobly designed. *The angels in you want out.* Give them exits and doorways through your acceptance and belief in continued and increasing good. It is only in the attitude of the conscious mind that we repress or express; and as I have already indicated, if we do repress, the expression will come anyway but it will come negatively. Repress the angels in your nature and devils will emerge, because devils are only dark angels, or the constructive forces inverted.

Wasted Sympathy

IF YOU ARE BLESSED with a sympathetic disposition don't waste it on yourself. Nothing is more deadly than self-pity. Nothing will withhold the blessings of life more surely than the tendency to brood over your misfortunes or the habit of constantly reminding yourself of how shabbily life has treated you.

The self-pitying individual is always giving himself an excellent treatment for lack. For it is the state of man's consciousness that is always demonstrated in his affairs. The consciousness of the man who feels sorry for himself is forever outpicturing more of the conditions which make him sad.

The cure, of course, is in a change of consciousness. A change of consciousness is made in this way: Take your attention from that which hurts and put it on that which would bless. Call the feeling of actually possessing the blessing until it changes your mood from sadness to joy. Keep this up and very soon your consciousness will change and you will see a corresponding change in your world.

Suffering for Another

ONE OF THE MOST PERSISTENT changes that afflict the lives of human beings is death. As the now silent voice of a popular news program of years ago used to say, "Today, as it does to all men, death came to so-and-so." Now, for those who die one of two things is true. Either they are in total oblivion and therefore without pain or sorrow or suffering, or they are freed of the frustrations of earthly life and are beginning to embrace a new experience with a fresh start. But it is the ones who are left behind who suffer. And for them I have a viewpoint which is helpful in time of death.

I first found this viewpoint years ago when I was returning from the cemetery where we had laid to rest the body of a great physician and a beloved man. I sat beside the widow along with the rest of the family in the back seat of the limousine as we drove away. And she said to me, "I am glad that I am the survivor and can bear this sorrow for him." At first I was struck with the magnificence and the utter nobility of this woman's statement and I admired her silently. Later I came to see how in her attitude she was lifting the burden from her own heart and alleviating her own sorrow and pain. For whenever we have a meaning in our suffering, it is more bearable. To feel that you are doing this for somebody else sort of takes the pain out of pain and the suffering out of suffering and makes the whole process something creative and meaningful. It is an old idea and I saw it put to work grandly that day and many times since.

We have all heard at one time or another of vicarious suffering. The word vicarious means "acting for another" or "suffering instead of someone else." History is full of examples but of course the one that comes to mind most readily is Jesus of Nazareth and the old Christian doctrine which says that he suffered and died upon the cross in order that the rest of us might be free and saved. Now, whatever this may mean to the theologians, it does not mean much to the average person, I find, because he does not understand it in terms of the practical. But there is great relief and inspiration, even joy, in the thought that the suffering somebody else might be having, you are having instead—for them. This gives meaning to suffering, and where there is meaning there is strength and the ability to endure.

Here is another example of what I mean. I found it in a little book which came to me the other day from England containing the broadcast talks of C. A. Joyce, a popular program in the morning hours on the BBC. The author says, "A very dear friend of mine suffered the loss of his wife. They were absolutely one in almost everything; they never did things apart and they did not exist independently at all. Then she died and my friend was desolate. In discussing his situation with Mr. Joyce, this husband said 'This is *my* way of helping *her*. You see, I am quite lost and bewildered; I am terribly upset and at times I break down and feel that the bottom has fallen out of life; there is nothing to live for any more. Then I try to remember that I am being selfish—I am thinking about *my* sorrow and *my* misery and *my* unhappiness and loneliness—but look: suppose I had died first. Then the person I love most would have to go through all this instead of me. *She* would be unhappy—*she* would be lonely and *she* would be feeling that the music of life would have stopped for *her*. Oh, I couldn't wish that, could I; all my life I've wanted to save her worry and being unhappy, and now isn't that what I want still? Of course. So I must try to remember that anything I suffer would have been hers. I would rather it were mine to save her. The more I suffer the more I know what she would have gone through and I couldn't wish that to an enemy—much less to one I love best of all. So I must bear it, not as something done to me but as something that might have been done to her—and God forbid.' "

Doesn't that take some of the sting out of death? And doesn't it put meaning into one's suffering? So often when people suffer loss and sink into their grief they say, "I don't care any more. Life for me is over. I am lonely and desolate and completely lost" or, as one person confided to me, "God is implacable, He is uncaring, he is unresponsive." But at that particular moment this person was thinking only of his own loss and not in terms of how this grief of his could be seen as bearing the load for another or instead of another. Prolonged grief for a departed one is always selfish for it indicates that we are thinking more about our own loss and our own suffering than we are of the release and the freedom of the one who has gone on.

These two accounts I have cited are of events which took place far removed from each other—one here in New York City and the other in England. Now we shall go to Vienna for another example which shows how universal is this principle or idea of suffering for another and how universal is its application. Dr. Victor Frankl tells of it in his book *Man's Search for Meaning*. Dr. Frankl spent three years in Auschwitz, the concentration camp, and underwent all of its horrors and came out bigger and stronger than before because he kept the meaning of Nietzsche's statement before him, "A man can stand almost any 'how' if he has a 'why.' "

Some years after Dr. Frankl had learned the meaning of this, an old physician and friend came to see him. The old gentleman had lost his wife and he was disconsolate. Dr. Frankl said to him, "Suppose you had died first and your wife were now alive." "Oh," said the old man, "I would not want that. She could not have borne it." "Well, then," replied Dr. Frankl, "don't you see that you are bearing that grief for her and that you are helping her by making it unnecessary that she should ever have to bear this grief?" That did it! It gave meaning to the old physician's suffering. Silently he rose, took the hand of his friend and fellow-physician and departed. He had found meaning, and whenever any of us finds meaning, there is more peace in our lives and in the world.

Not Peace
But a Sword

WE ALL HAVE a goal of finding peace in this constantly changing world. And having said that—that our goal is peace—I'm now going to deny it and advise not peace but a sword. That is, I shall *seem* to deny it, because I am referring to that arresting line in the sayings of Jesus which goes like this, "I came not to bring peace but a sword." This is not only arresting. It is confusing and contradictory and illogical. How can he who is called the Prince of Peace say this? How can the divine prototype and the divine example of what all men should be advise taking up the sword instead of bringing peace? The answer to all of these questions is part of the secret science of the Bible. Many of the discoveries of modern psychology are really rediscoveries of a more ancient science which is written in parable and symbolic sayings. For example, "I came not to bring peace but a sword" is a way of saying that disturbance, unrest and division are necessary to growth. Jesus represents the ideal man, and when the ideal in any degree comes to your mind it brings unrest and disturbance, and if you wish to move upward into the realization of that ideal you will have to make war against your old habits of thinking and acting.

Thus we can read this statment in this way: *I came not to bring peace but division*—division in the mind between what ails it and what will cure it. The sword is the symbol of division because it cuts and severs. Just as every human body must be severed from its parent body by a sword or a cutting edge, so every human mind has to be severed from its past by constructive thought and action. Psychiatrists and psychologists are always busy trying to wean grown men and women away from mama, and they discover that mom is still ruling and governing, and these grown men and women are still whining infants wanting mama. So the psychic cord between child and mother is not as readily cut as the physical cord is. But there is another kind of psychic cord that Jesus is speaking about in this line "I came not to bring peace but a sword." Be glad if you're disturbed, be glad you do not like it, because if you do not like it enough, you will move away from it. You will cleave to something else, first in your thought and then in your action and so you will make progress. So disturbance always precedes growth.

In another place we read, "If I had not come, they had not had sin." This "I" who speaks in this passage is the divine prototype of what every man should be, the ideal of the mind, the hope, its desire, its growing edge. If this does not come and present itself as a possibility to the mind, the mind will still feel satisfied with what it is and what it has been doing, and being satisfied it will have no disturbance and therefore it will take no action. Each time you become aware of something better and more desirable, you are disturbed and in need of division. Here's a rather simple illustration of this principle. You buy a new car or a new refrigerator or a new television or whatever and for a year or two you are quite happy with it until the new models come out. If you look at them and become fascinated with all of their new gadgetry, you become dissatisfied with your old machine. This is division and disturbance, and if it is great enough it will move you to buy a new machine. Because you are in sin, to use the biblical word. Something more ideal has come and spoken to you. And this situation cannot go on. There are only two things for it—either you adjust your thinking and satisfaction with your present machine or you get a new one. In either case the sword of division must be used.

Again, the divine man or the divine mind says, "He that saveth his life shall lose it and he that loseth his life for my sake shall find it." In other words, he that hangs on and is inflexible and will not allow himself to be disturbed by new hopes and new dreams and new ways of doing things cannot rise above his old level. He is what we used to call a stick-in-the-mud. He stays there; and staying there, he does not grow but rather deteriorates so that he loses his life.

What is your life? Your life is your state of mind, or rather your whole state of consciousness—the sum of your thought and feeling. Do you feel sad or happy? That is your life. Do you feel prosperous or poor? That is your life. We are not talking about your somatic or biological life, you see. We are talking about your consciousness because that is where you live. Do you feel confident or weak? That is your life. Whatever your psychological state is, that is your life as you are now living it, and sometimes it is a good idea to lose it so that you may take up a better life. And therefore the divine mind points out a pattern for our human minds to follow: "He that loseth his life for my sake, shall find it." Notice this phrase, "for my sake." That refers not to the man Jesus, not to the historical figure, but rather to the Christ indwelling in every man. What Paul describes as "Christ in you the hope of glory." When we lay down our morbid thought or fear or sadness we are not doing it for the sake of another person, either living or dead, and we are not doing it for the sake of God in Heaven. We are laying it down for the sake of developing a new level within ourselves and therefore a new man within ourselves, a man more like the divine pattern which is in us. Nobody can help God. Then why try to do anything for God's sake? God does not need help. God is the cosmic mind and beingness which is self-existent, whole, self-sustained and complete. Nothing can be added to that or taken from it. We do God no favor in thinking correctly or in acting admirably. No more can we do anything "for Christ's sake." We are not doing a favor for someone outside of ourselves or for the universe or for anything or anyone else. "For my sake" means for the sake of the development of the Christ which is largely dormant in each of us. Each time you make a constructive decision, you are developing your Christ. You are strengthening the image of yourself as a constructive, happy and healthful person.

Paul advises, "Let this mind be in you which was also in Christ Jesus." What was that mind? What was it like? We cannot tell, fully. No man is wise enough to define it completely. But for the purpose of the present we can project a tentative definition. The Christ mind is stable, confident and harmonious. That seems to say enough to set the Christ mind several notches above the best human mind that we know. The Christ mind is our potentiality. The Christ mind is our God-self. Now, each and every time we polarize our mind in stability and confidence and harmony, in accordance with these general principles, we are developing the Christ mind into more prominence and effectiveness in ourselves. Just as when we put a snapshot in the developing liquid and watch the image emerge out of nothing, so to speak. Every encounter with trouble, vexation, fear and inharmony in this earthly life is but a means whereby we develop the Christ in us. So we are doing it all "for Christ's sake." And he that loses his life by fear or weakness or inadequacy for Christ's sake is bringing in the sword of division and dividing the bad from the good.

We often lose our old life in a moment of diversion or entertainment or excitement but after the excitement is over we return to our old life again. The polarization has not been completely broken. The sword has not completely severed. There are all sorts of ways whereby people lose their life not "for Christ's sake" but for a moment of diversion or surcease or some other temporary relief. The alcoholic does it with alcohol, the pill-taker does it with an aspirin or a tranquilizer or pot, the disappointed and unsatisfied one does it with food, the hymn-singer does it with religious fervor, another does it with deep meditation and experiences a euphoria which he takes for the God-consciousness. In one way or another, most of us are running away, but the Hound of Heaven is on our trails and there is no real diversion or peace until "Christ be formed in you." To lose one's life "for my sake" is to want, above all things, the best and the highest operating majestically and triumphantly in one's life. And he who wants it with all of his heart will get it.

You Can Find Peace

ONE OF THE POETS affirms that peace is rarely denied to the peaceful. This saying "lays it right on the line." For it is a fundamental principle that the conditions one experiences are the results of one's state of consciousness. If one is peaceful then one has peace. Therefore, let us spend some time considering how to become peaceful.

Let us keep in mind that we are not talking philosophy or preaching religion merely. This is the science of thought and it embodies proven principles. Should one want proof of the fact that peace comes to the peaceful, let him consider everyday human relations. A sour disposition always provokes quarrels. Inharmonious feelings within oneself rub other people the wrong way. If you get out of bed on the wrong side and leave your home with a chip on your shoulder, it is almost inevitable that you will quarrel before ten o'clock. Feelings of inferiority or conceit or anxiety always produce adverse reactions from other people. But the person of humble calmness moves serenely through the day irrespective of the people and the conditions he meets. It is inward disturbance that causes outward disturbance, and all of one's philosophy and one's religion should lead toward the practice of inward calm and assurance. In the healings of Jesus we see this principle evidenced repeatedly. In nearly all of the healings of Jesus recorded in the New Testament it is made plain that a lack of peace inside an individual has caused his distress and his illness. Luke tells us in the fourth chapter that Jesus healed a man in the synagogue—a man "with an unclean devil." This simply means that the man's mind was temporarily deranged. Having an unclean devil means that the man was dirty in his thinking, not dirty in an obscene way but dirty in the sense that principles and ideas were confused in his mind. There was no purity of thinking, no consciousness of thought, no incisiveness of decision. Desires and anxieties, inferiorities and conceits, guilts and ambitions were all at sixes and sevens in the man's mind and he was not able to put each one in its proper place, to give each one no more than its allotted portion of attention. His ideas and opinions were calling up irrational emotions which, like so many compulsive forces, were driving him first this way and then the other.

We have two levels of mind: the conscious or rational level, and the subconscious or irrational level. The subconscious is the seat of the emotions. The thoughts and opinions and concepts of the conscious mind when based upon Truth keep the subconscious waters in their place and everything moves in divine law and order. But when the ideas and concepts of the conscious mind are based on error, then the gates are left open and the subconscious irrationality floods up and over the rational mind, and this is mental derangement or nervous breakdown or an unclean devil. In healing the individual, Jesus spoke directly to this unclean devil and said, "Hold thy peace and come out of him." In other words, the Master Consciousness said to irrational consciousness, "Be still. Return to your own level, and do not intrude where you do not belong." It is often amazing how speaking thus with authority to an irrational movement of mind you can inhibit and silence that movement and bring peace to the mind.

It is written that Jesus "suffered not the devils to speak." He did not parley with evil. He did not analyze and discuss. Evil can always make a good case for itself if you allow it to talk. The case will sound so plausible and reasonable that the mind will begin to accept it and lose its ability to deal with the problem. Reasons can always be found for one's suffering. Self-justification then sets in and this is deadly. If you want peace of mind and healing, do not allow this process to begin. Follow Jesus and "suffer not the devils to speak." Do not tolerate error. Do not accept evil or limitation. Of course, you have to accept the reality of your present suffering, but do not accept a vision of its continuance. Discussion only reinfects the mind. Substitute Truth for error. Return good for evil and that is the end of evil.

Again Luke tells us in chapter seven that a sinful woman was washing Jesus' feet in the house of Simon, the rich man. All the assembled company knew she was a sinner and murmured among themselves because Jesus would have anything to do with her. He said to this woman, "Thy faith hath saved thee. Go in peace." In other words, here again is the recognition that the trouble with this woman was an inward quarrel. This is always the cause of immorality, indecency or crime. A person who is whole within himself is whole in his relationships with other people and his environment.

In the fifth chapter of Mark we read that to the woman who had an issue of blood and who touched his garment in the throng Jesus said, "Daughter, thy faith hath made thee whole. Go in peace and be whole of thy plague." Here is a case of physical sickness, and it too is caused by a lack of peace in the consciousness. In these three instances in the Scriptures, each one of the sick is sick in a different way, yet Jesus recognizes that every one is sick because he has some inward quarrel or division and therefore lack of peace within. Each in his own way is at odds with life, with people, with the times, with events, with his own guilts and frustrations and desires and hopes. Each one has in some way forgotten his union with God, the Infinite and the Whole; each one has valued himself as less than the conditions which seem to be arrayed against him.

It is good to examine oneself frequently. Most of us do not know our own faults and personality failings. Pride and the terrific thrust of the human ego tend to hide them from us. Therefore it is necessary to earnestly entreat the inner Knower to inform us, to guide us.

But do not carry self-analysis too far. Be synthetic. *Synthetic* means to put things together. If one is lacking in peace within oneself, it means that the wrong elements are in consciousness —the elements of warfare and division. Some knowledge of what is wrong is always good, but in general it is better to put the right elements in than to war against the bad elements in order to expel them. If you have a pail of dirty water, you can turn it upside down and empty the dirty water all at once. But this will make a mighty big splash and unless you are out-of-doors, you may have a mess on your hands. Also you might not be able to lift the pail of water. There is another way of emptying it and that is by putting it under the faucet and letting clean water run into it. You can even change a pail of dirty water to clean water with an eyedropper if you have the patience. Putting clean water into dirty will gradually transform and cleanse the whole vessel. It is so with the mind. Keep putting the right things in, and the mind and the whole consciousness will be transformed.

This is one of the reasons why religious practice of all kinds and of all ages has generally prescribed morning and evening prayer. In the morning before you go forth, lift your thoughts to the truth of your union with God, and continuing therefrom, conclude that you are strong, capable, illumined, wise, peaceful, and all that you do this day will prosper. Clothe yourself in your divine nature and go forth so clothed. At evening examine your conscience and forgive yourself the errors that loom there by acknowledging the mistakes but noting what the right way should be and resolving to follow it hereafter. If your inner self accuses you of any mistake, do not go to sleep until you have forgiven yourself by giving, in exchange for the guilt, a constructive resolve and a calm assurance for success the next day. You might also want to do this several times during the day but morning and evening are absolutely essential if you want to build elements of peace into the inward consciousness and so follow out the poet's observation that, "peace is rarely denied to the peaceful."

They are peaceful who have the elements of peace integrated into their character and nature. The means of integration are, in part, as we have here described. Be ruthless in your thought; turn it to the great truths and allow your sympathy to engage these. Image yourself as being right and true, courageous and faithful, prosperous and loving, and as receiving love from others and being in harmony with all things and with all people and with all processes and all elements. Do this in spite of your predicament. Do it in spite of the way you feel. The way to pray effectively is to invoke the mood of being or having that which you want, even when all of your sensations are just the opposite to this.

Practice unclothing yourself of your old opinions upon whatever subject and going naked before the Divine Spirit, willing to be clothed according to its will. Do it often—do it at least morning and evening and you will be at peace with yourself and with the whole world.

Be Willing to
Have It So

THE REASON THAT CHANGE is so difficult for a great
many people is that they remain rigid in their opinions. We have
heard it said that the Empire State Building sways as much as
twelve inches off the vertical in a high wind. Its flexible core of
steel enables it to do this. Were it too rigid, it would snap and
break. With people it is rigidity of attitude and opinion which
causes them to suffer when the turbulence of the world touches
them. Someone says something that makes you smart. Another
accepts your favor and never returns a word of thanks. Someone
dies and suddenly the whole world is dark as night. Some plan
or prospect you set your heart upon turns to ashes overnight and
the abomination of desolation creeps into the human heart.

All of these and many more like them are called the circumstances of change; no one can foresee them all; no one can stop
them all. One can only react. And if one overreacts, he may burn
himself up. If he underreacts, he may be overwhelmed. How
does one handle these situations expertly with the least amount
of suffering and the greatest amount of profit? William James

170

gave the world a formula. He said: "Be willing to have it so." That does not mean acceptance and resignation. Rather, it means intelligent and constructive reaction and forward movement in spite of momentary shock and change. "Be willing to have it so."

So you stubbed your toe. Don't argue with the fact. You cannot change that fact. It is already past history. Don't fuss and fume because the world is not the world as you would have it be. It is as it is. Be willing to have it so. Don't fight the problem. Don't argue with the event. Hold you breath, brace yourself and let the wave of the world break over you. Once it has spent its force it is afterward harmless. Then you can proceed to do something constructive about the problem.

The one big problem of life is friction. Whether in engineering a machine or in learning how to live, the goal is to achieve and move forward with as little friction as possible. Rub your finger along the tabletop and it gets hot because the tabletop offers resistance to the movement of the finger. Put a little oil on the end of your finger, and it will glide freely with much less friction. That is why the king of men is called the Anointed for he is made smooth and frictionless by the anointing oil of wisdom and the healing ointment of truth. And the divine voice encourages "them that mourn in Zion" to receive "beauty for ashes, the oil of joy for mourning, the garment of praise for the spirit of heaviness."

How does friction arise in our mental and emotional lives before it ever manifests in our social lives? It arises through the confrontation of events and circumstances by our fixed opinions. All men have ideals and the crude world does not always match their ideals. The result is friction and suffering. Shall a man then give up his ideals and never stand for what is right or good and let the ugly and the crude ride roughshod over him? No, but he shall realize that an ideal is the gift of God. It is the intrusion into the individual mind of a promise from the universal mind and there are more ways of fulfilling that ideal than the individual mind often supposes. Let a person realize this and fit himself to become a channel for something bigger than himself. He will become an instrument then of divine forces which will move him with less friction to accomplish that which he deems right and good.

During the Depression a friend of a friend of mine lost all he had. He was a newpaper man and with his last five dollars he bought a dozen roses and brought them home to his wife. His family were all shocked and depressed by the events but he alone was not. He took out of his pocket the stub of a pencil with which he used to report and write, and said, "Cheer up, my dears, so long as I have this pencil and your love, we'll make it." And make it they did. The thing had happened and he was willing to have it so and to go on. He could have fought the situation, cursed the darkness. Instead he lit a little light. He was flexible enough to bend when the blow fell. But he did not give way. He did not agree with the event and accept its suggestion of loss and destruction. He remained flexible and bent and gave way but agreed with life and accomplishment and happiness, and what he agreed with he found.

Those who insist that the world conform to their view are usually broken or at the very least suspended and stranded. Take the new sailor who tries to withstand the rising and the falling of the deck beneath him. He gets seasick. He soon learns, however, to adapt his walking to the rhythm of the sea and the deck beneath him, and that is why every sailor throughout history has a rolling gait. There is a way to do everything with the least amount of friction. As Solomon the Wise says: There is a time for everything under the sun. When everything is happy and going smoothly, it is a time to rejoice and to be merry and to enjoy the hour. If the hour that follows is perilous and threatening and circumstances are not happy, then it is a time for standing still in regard to outer events and a time for moving within with attitudes and moods.

Here is a rule I have found helpful through the years: When your trouble is in the outside world such as the threat and the pressure of events, then stand still and adjust your thoughts by thinking the highest truth you know and rejoicing in it. When you get your mind and heart in order, the outside world will be more frictionless. When the trouble is inside yourself such as a vexed and disordered mind, don't bother about your thoughts but move boldly out into the world and become involved with people and things and events. Your depression will soon pass.

I repeat: When the trouble is outside, go within, adjust your thinking. When the trouble is inside, go outside, get involved. With this little formula, you can ride out the turbulence of any kind of difficulty and come bravely into the haven of peace.

How the Dead Rise

AN OLD FRIEND of mine, now graduated from this life
for many years, once stood looking at the sunset over her beloved waters of Maine and composed these lines which she entitled *Sunset and Sunrise*:

> Flaming red and brilliant blue,
> Orange, purple, royal hue.
> God's pageantry—
> Bearing triumphantly those souls
> Who left our earth today
> To reach their higher goals.
> Say not, 'They rest in peace.'
> When comes the morn
> They live again, new-born.

How many are the sentiments like this both in prose and in
poetry written by generations past and which will be written by
generations yet to come to voice their belief in immortality or
the continuity of human life! Yet there is no proof that it is true.
One must add in the same breath, however, that there is no
proof that continuity is not true. Humanity is divided into those

174

who believe and those who do not believe. Each stoutly affirms his conviction but neither can marshal proof in its behalf. I frequently recall a sheep rancher in Idaho who said to me: "See that sheep over there? When it's dead, it's dead; and it's the same with you and me." He was just as positive as those who believe. But he had no proof. As usual with opposites, the truth lies somewhere in between. There is something about a man which perishes. There is something about a man which is imperishable. Each of us judges by what he sees. Both sides are right but each judges by his own light and by the evidence which is available to him.

We have never seen a dead body revivified. Bodies die and change into their basic elements. Eyes which recognized and were recognized close, and lips which spoke are silent. This much perishes. And if a man be all contained within this leathern bag we call our body, then there is an end to him; and our faith, as Paul says, is vain. But there are certain other evidences about this matter which both sides of the question would do well to take into account. How often is death falsely reported? And those to whom it is so reported suffer all the pangs and sorrows of grief and loss attendant upon that news. This happens most frequently in wartime. A soldier's death is reported, and those who knew and loved him are shocked and hurt and bereft. Then comes a correct report: he is not dead at all but was falsely reported so, and then those to whom the report comes rejoice and laugh and are gay again. In such a situation death was entirely a mental experience with no foundation in fact.

Suppose such a false report of death came to you? When did you suffer? When the news came. When did you cease to suffer? When the truth was made known to you. Yet all the while there was no change in events. The changes were entirely within you. To you the person was dead. To himself he was quite alive. We judge all things by the evidence which is presented to us, and according to our judgment we suffer or rejoice. Thus there can be a kind of death to one who believes with a little evidence or with the wrong evidence. Who can say, then, that the evidence by which the vast majority of mankind judges is sufficient or that it adequately reflects the truth of the matter? Death may be in us, the so-called living, and not in those we call dead. If the heart is right and the instinct speaks truly, then this is surely the case.

The idea of death is an impression in consciousness which may be wholly unrelated to actual fact. Here is a way of looking at it. One may observe that he has many present perceptions which were once "dead" in him. As a child you did not think as you do now. What you are now aware of was once dormant or unawakened or "dead." Life is a continual growth in awareness. Possibilities and capacities and strengths which were once buried and inactive rise into consciousness and increase the range and meaning of the personality. There is a good deal of buried life in each and every one of us seeking resurrection or activation. In the unconscious depths of every person are strengths and meanings and miracles waiting to be brought to the surface. Oftentimes we have flashes of insight as when a watcher of the water sees a flash or a shadow and knows that life swims far below.

He who begins to have some apprehension of the vast subconscious life that lies beneath the threshold of ordinary consciousness, or begins to feel himself in depth, will respond with new insight to the announcement of the Scripture, "As Moses lifted up the serpent in the wilderness even so must the Son of man be lifted up." He will recognize that there is something in each one of us that crawls and creeps; that has no backbone; it is sinuous and afraid of the light. This dim dream of power must be lifted up until it can stand alone and walk abroad in majesty and beauty instead of crawling and creeping before the events and sensations of the world.

Here is a humorous account of a commonplace experience, and it illustrates how the buried life of a child rises into consciousness, perception, and action. A small boy was a compulsive thumb-sucker. Every known method of reward and punishment had been used to cure him. His parents had tied the thumb, they had soaked it in bitter aloes, they had slapped him, they had withheld candy and they had given him candy—all with no effect. He continued to suck the thumb and the habit grew firmer and firmer until by the age of six he was a public spectacle. One day he suddenly stopped the habit. When his astonished parents asked why, he simply replied, ''Big boys don't suck their thumbs.'' From somewhere, insight had come to him. The old habit died then and there and a higher manner of life was born or resurrected. That which had previously crawled as an unconscious possibility now stood up as a conscious perception and function. It helps in this connection to observe that the Greek meaning of the word resurrect means to ''stand up.''

There is buried life in each of us. It is this that the Scriptures refer to as Christ or ''Christ in you the hope of glory.'' It is this buried life in each man that is portrayed in the Scriptures as Christ rising from the dead. For the majority of believers the resurrection story is the account of Jesus, the Son of God, falsely accused by evil men, cruelly crucified and buried but rising miraculously from the grave to be seen again in bodily form. But to others, with a different kind of insight, the story describes the fact that there is in every person a buried greatness; an infinite possibility and a promised majesty which is falsely accused by the mind's false beliefs and foolish notions, killed by doubt and fear, thrust back by anger and wayward emotion and finally buried in spiritual ignorance. ''He is despised and rejected of men . . . we esteemed him not.''

If you as a person know your growing spiritual power over

every trial and burden of this life, you are dying as a drudge, as a man of sorrow and becoming a person of confidence and assurance and peace. It is a becoming process only from a sense standpoint. Actually and truly you always were whatever you will become. What is seen as growth is really an unfoldment or an evolution of a former involution.

Sometimes the change in a person is dramatic. Old friends come to see you and cannot find the person you once were. They will seek you in your old body, in the grave of your old habits among "the dead" of your old cerebral and physical movements, but they will not find you. Something in you will say to them as it was said of old, "Why seek ye the living among the dead?"

If a Man Die

IF A MAN DIE shall he live again?

Yes, unquestionably. Better still, he continues to live without interruption. Only that which was born can die. The body was born, and the body can die. The Spirit was never born and will never die. The Spirit is God and God cannot die. Being imperishable, all that it learns and knows is imperishable too. It uses a body as an instrument. Only through the body can the Spirit act and work on this plane. It is never absorbed by its body. It is always transcendent of its environment. It is always at home wherever it is. Some body it will always have, for body is necessary to expression.

Death is more than an end. It is also a beginning. Where something ends, something also begins. There cannot be one without the other. What this new beginning is, no one can tell. All efforts to describe it must remain as speculation. But we know that "life goes not backward nor tarries with yesterday." So it must be progress, newness, freedom. The universe is law and order and continual growth. While the human mind may never answer the questions of where and why, it must and shall take comfort in the whispering of the heart: "It must be good or it would not be."